Conscious Parenting

Insights and Wisdom from a Veteran Kindergarten Teacher

John F. Ledgar

First published by Ultimate World Publishing 2025
Copyright © 2025 John Ledgar

ISBN

Paperback: 978-1-923425-07-1
Ebook: 978-1-923425-08-8

John Ledgar has asserted his rights under the Copyright, Designs and Patents Act 1988 to be identified as the author of this work. The information in this book is based on the author's experiences and opinions. The publisher specifically disclaims responsibility for any adverse consequences which may result from use of the information contained herein. Permission to use information has been sought by the author. Any breaches will be rectified in further editions of the book.

All rights reserved. No part of this publication may be reproduced, stored in or introduced into a retrieval system, or transmitted in any form, or by any means (electronic, mechanical, photocopying, recording or otherwise) without the prior written permission of the author. Any person who does any unauthorised act in relation to this publication may be liable to criminal prosecution and civil claims for damages. Enquiries should be made through the publisher.

Cover design: Ultimate World Publishing
Layout and typesetting: Ultimate World Publishing
Editor: Victoria Pickens

Ultimate World Publishing
Diamond Creek,
Victoria Australia 3089
www.writeabook.com.au

Testimonials

As a mother of teenagers and a high school teacher, I have come to appreciate the vital role emotional intelligence plays in a child's development. The chapter on empowering emotional intelligence highlights practical ways to nurture emotional awareness and resilience from an early age, something I wish I had known when my children were in Kindergarten. The strategies outlined not only benefit young children but offer a foundation that will support them well into their teenage years and beyond. Highly recommended for any parent looking to build strong emotional connections with their child!
    Vandana Verma
    Secondary School Teacher

I have had the privilege of working with John in a kindergarten setting, and he is truly exceptional. His ability to connect with children and create a positive, engaging learning environment is remarkable. John tailors his teaching to meet the individual needs of each child, ensuring they are both challenged and supported. He fosters an atmosphere of respect, curiosity, and growth, making a lasting impact on every child he works with.

In addition to his outstanding teaching, John is a highly valued team member. He is collaborative, supportive, and always willing to share his knowledge and resources with his colleagues. John's positive attitude and strong work ethic contribute to a productive and harmonious work environment. His professionalism, commitment to excellence, and dedication to both children and colleagues make him an asset to any team. It has been a pleasure working with him.

Mona Sharma
Early Childhood Teacher

Through having the privilege of working with John as a preservice teacher, I found him to be exceptional with the children in the room, especially when they have been upset. He comforts the children in a very unique way by finding out what has upset them and working through the child's emotions with them. Through seeing how he has done this, I feel parents could learn a great deal from John and take his advice on board. I know that as I continue in my studies, I will take on what I have learnt from John and reach out to him for further advice and guidance.

Tammy Lovette
Preservice Teacher

As a parent who has gone through my child's transition to kindergarten, I found "Chapter 4: Separation Made Smoother" to be an invaluable resource. It highlights the significance of acknowledging feelings and offers practical strategies for tackling separation anxiety. I especially appreciated the advice on creating a quick goodbye routine, which made our departures much easier. Moreover, the insights into how trauma from the COVID-19 pandemic has affected children helped me gain a deeper understanding of my child's emotions. This perspective clarified why some of my approaches

Testimonials

resonate better than others. I highly recommend this book for both parents and educators!
Philip S, Parent

I have known, worked and had a friendship with John since 2013. John has always been very passionate about children's education and sharing his experience and knowledge with the Kindergarten Children in his care. To have written a book shows the dedication of his beliefs in this field.
I am sure his passion for the job and his love of further education will be a driving force in his life in years to come.
Good Luck
Maureen Taylor
Early Childhood Educator

Dedication

To the children who have taught me the beauty of curiosity, resilience, and play.

To the parents and carers who show unwavering love, patience, and devotion.

And to my own journey of growth and discovery, which has guided me to this moment.

May this book empower, illuminate, and inspire the path toward conscious and compassionate parenting.

With gratitude and love,
John F. Ledgar

Contents

Testimonials	iii
Dedication	vii
Preface	xi
Foreword	xiii
Disclaimer	xv
Introduction	1
The Magic of Kindergarten	7
Ready, Set, Kindergarten!	15
Kindergarten – New Beginnings	27
Separation Made Smoother	37
The Power of Playtime	47
Empowering Emotional Intelligence	59
Nurturing Positive Behaviour	73
Nourishing Through Nutritious Choices	91
Cultivating Restful Sleep Habits	105
Conclusion	113
About the Author	115
Acknowledgements	117
References	121
Speaker Bio	125
Special Offers	127

Preface

During the last term of 2022, I found myself reflecting on the common concerns and support needs parents often shared with me. Inspired by these conversations, I began preparing a series of workshops designed to address these topics. My passion for writing and supporting others sparked a dream: to transform these workshops into a book.

One evening, someone asked me if I was writing a book or if I had ever written one. The next day, during a casual conversation with my sister, I shared this question with her. Her simple yet powerful response was, "What's holding you back?"

That question lingered with me. It gave me the nudge I needed, and the very next day I wrote the first chapter.

This book is the culmination of my journey as a kindergarten teacher, drawing upon over twenty-five years of experience in the education sector. It is a blend of practical advice, insights, and heartfelt reflections designed to support parents and caregivers in raising confident and resilient children.

You can choose to read this book cover to cover or skip to the sections that are most relevant to your current challenges and interests.

I hope this book becomes a trusted resource for you and brings value to your parenting journey.

Warm regards,
John F. Ledgar

Foreword

I first met John in 2002 when he and I were working in a long day care centre kindergarten room. He was the new graduate teacher; I was his support educator. Back then he was enthusiastic, willing to learn all he could so he could grow as a teacher. After I moved on from that service and furthered my studies to also become a kindergarten teacher, we reconnected 10 years later over social media and I was thrilled to see he was still teaching and his knowledge and passion for this sector had continued to grow. We have stayed in touch, chatted many times and shared our joint commitment to not only support the staff and children we work with but their families too. With over 20 years of teaching experience, John brings a wealth of understanding to families of what to expect when your child starts Kindergarten. He has a deep understanding of the worries that families present with when their child is enrolled; this is often the first time a child has been in the care of strangers and it's often a vulnerable time for families. It's also an incredibly important part of the development of a child where they are taking some steps towards independence and forming relationships with other trusted adults and their friends. It's truly a privilege to be in this role as a teacher or educator as we support the whole family to trust this process and see your child grow and thrive. Sometimes early interventions may be required to help your child develop and grow, but we have the knowledge and skills to ensure the appropriate supports are in place to help your child. Our focus is child centred, and we want each child to have the best early education learning experience they can have before heading into the structured learning of school. John's book covers many topics that consistently come up in the early stages of the kindergarten journey and he will answer the questions you may have as well as sharing the expectations of this stage in your child's early education journey in a compassionate and knowledgeable way. I wish you and your child the very best as they embark on this beautiful and exciting adventure into kindergarten.

Beck Cowley
Bachelor of Teaching (Birth to 5 Years)
Masters of Special Education and Inclusion

Disclaimer

The opinions shared in this book are my own, drawn from twenty-five years of experience as well as the various professional development opportunities and training I have undertaken. These views are intended as an invitation for you to reflect, ponder, and determine how they may align with your own understanding and beliefs.

To protect the privacy of the individuals mentioned, all names included in the chapters have been changed.

If you have specific concerns about your child and do not find the solutions you seek within these pages, I strongly encourage you to consult with your child's Maternal and Child Health Nurse, Kindergarten Teacher, or Paediatrician.

Introduction

My journey to becoming a qualified Kindergarten Teacher began way back when I first went to university. Teaching was never on my agenda. When I initially decided to go to university, my goal was to study and then join the Australian Federal Police.

I had previously applied for the Victoria Police, but I did not pass the spelling component of the entrance exam. Then, I decided to investigate joining the Army. Finally, I began leaning towards joining the Federal Police, for which I needed a University Qualification.

I investigated Degrees, including Behavioural Science, Psychology and finally landed on a Bachelor of Arts, where I could study Psychology, Sociology, and Politics (to name a few). Finally, the day came when I received confirmation that I had been accepted into La Trobe University, Bendigo. The enrolment day was the same day I was due to sign up for the Army. I like to think that divine intervention guided me down the path that eventually led me to becoming an Early Childhood Teacher, or more commonly known as a Kindergarten Teacher.

When I commenced my studies, I enrolled in Psychology, Sociology, Politics and Geography.

I have always been fascinated by the human condition, particularly the psychology of the mind and how consciousness works. University gave me an opportunity to explore this further.

Struggling with my studies, as well as the allure of living away from my parents, I did not do very well in my Bachelor of Arts.

Many times, throughout my two years living in Bendigo, friends would say to me that I should transfer into Education and do Teaching. Something I ignored as I thought it was a lot of work.

Finally, after two years in Bendigo, I transferred to Monash University Clayton, where I completed my Bachelor of Arts with a Major in History and sub majors in Sociology, Politics, and Geography. In retrospect, and to paraphrase the great Bruce Lee, my Bachelor of Arts taught me to think deeply about unemployment.

After completing my Bachelor of Arts, I did a lot of casual manual labour and did not see much of a future. I was disheartened until a friend told me about an integration aide program through the Work for the Dole program.

I applied and began working as a volunteer teacher's aide at a Primary School. This led to a paid position doing a reading

Introduction

recovery position called 'Bridging the Gap' which I ran for eighteen months before the role became redundant.

This was when I began looking into Teaching as a viable future, as I could see the benefits of teaching and the support I could offer students. After applying for both Primary and Early Childhood Education courses, I was accepted into Monash University to undertake my Graduate Diploma of Early Childhood Education.

For the first time in my life, I was getting good grades. Averaging between a Credit and a Distinction, I completed my course two years later and was able to walk straight into my first role, with a service I had undertaken my last placement, at the beginning of 2003.

Though my studies had taught me a lot, I was still a small fish in a big pond. I dove in the deep end, and somehow I managed to swim. I spent the next ten years in various age groups in a Childcare Centre.

After around seven years, I decided I needed a new challenge. I went back to university and undertook my third qualification, the Graduate Diploma of Primary Education. This gave me an insight into how education looks in a school setting. There were some things that I really liked and took back with me to the Childcare Centre I worked at.

After almost ten years in Childcare, I landed a position as a Kindergarten Teacher at a Local Council Kindergarten and began the role I had been dreaming of for a long time.

My first year in this role was very challenging. Lots of new learning and navigating the extended breaks that Kindergarten

Teachers have during the term holidays. It was the first time I'd had mentoring in my role as a teacher and I learnt a lot from these staff and really appreciated their time and effort.

It took me another ten years working with this local council, for me to undertake the training that changed everything. Due to the release of the School Readiness Funding (SRF) I was able to undertake the 'Tuning into Kids®' facilitator training and become a 'Tuning into Kids®' Facilitator. This taught me so much about emotional intelligence, emotion coaching and the impact an adult's response to the emotions of a child can have on the child.

This training fit very well with my own philosophy of teaching children.

Believing that every child is unique and have their own strengths and interests. That the family are a child's first and most important teacher, and I, as a Teacher, am but a facilitator to support the work that families have already been doing, to empower parents and to increase their innate capacities.

Working closely with and establishing strong relationships with parents and their children is a recurring theme in my annual work appraisals. This has even led to my deployment to locations where many families and children were at risk and required extra support and understanding.

Sitting here, writing this, when I think back to my days at university in Bendigo, I never would have dreamt that I would become a teacher. However, it was one of the best decisions I ever made, and I particularly love the relationships I have built with families, children, and colleagues throughout the years.

Introduction

In this book you will discover some of the tips I have offered to families throughout my years as a Kindergarten Teacher. What I have discovered is that parents seek the similar sort of advice and support again and again, year in and year out. Every year would bring a new cohort of children and families. Every year the new cohort of parents would ask me the same questions I was asked the previous year. This pointed out to me that there is a need for a book such as this, which offers parents simple strategies to help them to tackle the intricacies of kindergarten and support their child to have an enjoyable experience at kindergarten and a successful start to their education.

The Magic of Kindergarten

Introduction

Kindergarten is a big experience, even for the most well-adjusted and developmentally ready child. It is a unique time of learning and discovery. In today's society, we have created an outcome perspective in which everything we do is aimed at a goal.

To quote Ralph Waldo Emerson: "It's not the destination, it's the journey."

When we do not pay attention to the journey, we miss a lot. Being fixated on the goal of getting your child ready for school can cause you to miss the many victories and achievements your child achieves throughout Kindergarten.

Your child's journey is their destination.

Significance of Kindergarten

Most children spend one year at Kindergarten. In 2024, Australia, children have universal access to early childhood education. This means they have access to 600 hours of Early Childhood Education in the year before school. 2020 saw the commencement of funded three-year-old Kindergarten in Victoria, giving most children access to two years of Funded Kindergarten.

This demonstrates the understanding of the importance of Early Childhood Education in children's learning and future potential.

However, we need to remember that Kindergarten is not just preparation for the future. Childhood is only a short period of time, and it is important to allow children to be children. In most cases, given an appropriate and supportive environment, children will develop, grow, and learn.

Likewise, Kindergarten needs to be embraced as an important moment in a child's life and embraced for its uniqueness.

Cherish the Now

Something I have come to understand during my career, is the importance of being in the moment. Embracing your child's childhood as a significant moment in time, not just as preparation for the future. Being open and curious to the how, not just the *why* of childhood.

Too often, I hear well-meaning parents tell me they want their child to learn to write their name, count, and know their colours. Often, this is about a child who is not able to hold a pencil correctly yet. I then explain to the parent that we incorporate literacy and numeracy into all aspects of the program in a play-based way that helps their child develop the appropriate skills for literacy and numeracy.

I have observed that many parents are focussed twelve or more months ahead and lose sight of the present moment in their child's life. Focusing on Kindergarten purely as a means for preparing a child for the future can set them up for failure if they do not reach a predetermined level. Whereas focussing on the present moment enables parents and teachers to be more responsive to the immediate needs of the child and cater the program and support to what the child needs the most in the moment.

When they enter school, children have approximately twelve years of formal education ahead of them. I believe we should allow children to be children and enjoy their time in kindergarten. We should encourage them to explore, make predictions, and make mistakes so they can become lifelong, inquisitive learners. By incorporating literacy, numeracy, science, music, and movement into the Kindergarten program, children are given the opportunity to explore the world around them in a way that complements their learning style.

For more information on learning styles see the chapter: *The Power of Playtime*.

When we focus on the journey, we can learn many things. When our focus is on a destination, we only learn achievement or failure. The journey is where all learning happens, whether that is learning new skills in Kindergarten such as how to socialise or negotiate, or skills beyond Kindergarten such as crossing the road, how to ride a bike and more. The journey is often the part we forget, whereas we remember the destination, for positive or negative reasons.

Help your child to remember their journey, for the journey will often continue to teach us, well beyond the destination we were aiming for.

Present Actions, Future Growth

Focusing on your child's development and learning in the moment has the added benefit of helping to prepare them for the future. By supporting their development and learning now, you are teaching them how to cope with and manage their learning later in life.

If you focus on getting your child ready for school, they may learn some of the necessities, such as reading, writing, or mathematical knowledge. However, they are likely to miss other important skills, such as negotiation, interpersonal skills, emotional knowledge, and resilience.

This is not to say that you cannot focus on the skills your child needs for school. It is, however, important to introduce those skills when your child has all the previous skills and attributes developed.

An example of this, is making your child practice writing their name. This is fine, if your child already has strong core strength, fine motor muscle strength and the ability to focus on detail. If they do not have these precursors to writing, then the task of writing will be much more difficult and less enjoyable for your child.

Instead, encourage your child to draw, use tongs or tweezers to sort small items, play with playdough or clay, lie on their stomach on the ground, on a cushion, to read a book. Get them to help carry heavy (for them) items around the house. All these activities will help to develop the core and fine motor strength your child needs to successfully learn to write their name.

When you focus on the now, you are laying the foundations for a solid life of learning. Just like laying the foundations for a building. The foundation needs to be solid to give your child the basis for lifelong learning.

Timing for Success

Many parents are concerned about whether their child is ready for Kindergarten. One of the best resources to draw upon, if you are unsure and your child is deferment age, is your Maternal and Child Health Nurse. If you are concerned, make an appointment, and explain you want to check their development and learning to see if they are ready.

The next point of call would be to approach your local Kindergarten and request a walk through. During this session, discuss your concerns with the Teacher. There are a few things to consider:

- Is there any developmental or learning delays?
- Is your child able to easily separate from you?
- Is your child emotionally and socially mature enough for their age?

For more information to help you decide if your child is ready for Kindergarten and strategies to help them get ready, please refer to the chapter: *Ready, Set, Kinder.*

If you have concerns and still want to proceed with Kindergarten, it is essential that you raise these concerns with your child's Kindergarten Teacher. In some cases, if a child meets a set of criteria, the Teacher can apply for Kindergarten Inclusion Support funding for the child.

On the other hand, many parents have requested a second year for their child, because they are young. Being young does not automatically qualify a child to meet the criteria of a Second Year Application. To qualify, a child needs to have delays in two or more of the developmental domains and has either had support from a Preschool Field Officer (PSFO) or be in early intervention. For more information you can speak to your child's Kindergarten Teacher.

If your child is young, born closer to the Kindergarten cutoff date (see your state or territory department for Kindergarten cut off dates), please consider whether they are ready. Starting Kindergarten before your child is ready, puts barriers in front of them from the start.

If we start children too early, they will always be playing catchup. We want children to be able to thrive when they start Kindergarten, and later, school.

While age is one aspect, it is also important to speak to your child's Teacher to ascertain if they fit the criteria, whether you are requesting support funding or a second year at Kindergarten. Your child's Teacher is the perfect person to inform you and help you with making an informed decision.

A note to mention to parents. When seeking advice from doctors, make sure that they are paediatric trained. I have experienced several times where families have disregarded the professional opinion of a Kindergarten Teacher because their GP said their child is fine. General Practitioner doctors are not necessarily trained in child development and do not have the same expertise as a Kindergarten Teacher or a Paediatrician in relation to child develop. If in doubt, request a referral for a Paediatrician or speak to your child's teacher about other referral pathways through the Allied Health services.

Conclusion

As parents, we often want to help our child to achieve milestones and progress, usually ahead of time. However, when we expect children to do things that they are not ready for, this creates a barrier for future development and learning.

If you have any concerns about your child's learning and development, speak to your Maternal and Child Health Nurse or your child's Kindergarten Teacher to find out where they are developmentally and whether there is any concern.

Focus on the present moment, support, and celebrate their immediate successes, and encourage them to continue to practice the skills they have already mastered, so that these can be the stepping stones to future skill development and become a lifelong learner.

Ready, Set, Kindergarten!

Introduction

With more than twenty years of experience working with young children, mainly in the three-to-five-year age bracket, I have seen many families struggling with settling their child into Kindergarten. One of the things I have learnt is that preparing your child for the transition into Kindergarten is an essential part of the journey.

In this chapter, parents will discover some easy strategies to help them prepare their child for Kindergarten and minimise the anxiety associated with separation that both children and parents face.

The Importance of Preparation

Consider this. You are dropped off in a foreign place, with limited or no ability to communicate. Your anxiety increases as you try to navigate this new world, whilst at the same time trying to learn to communicate. Your emotions are all over the place and you do not know what to do.

Some children face this experience when they begin Kindergarten, even if they have had preparation. Preparing your child for the transition to Kindergarten can help most children deal with the anxiety and uncertainty they feel when they are left in a new space without any familiar adults or people to comfort them.

Preparing your child can also decrease the duration of separation anxiety in children. Without adequate planning, the anxiety may persist for a long time and make the Kindergarten experience negative for your child. However, when they are well-equipped, the duration and intensity of the anxiety can be reduced and even eliminated entirely with regular attendance and support.

Preparation is the Key

As with anything we plan in life, preparation is the key. This is absolutely true when it comes to preparing your child for transition from home to childcare or the Kindergarten environment. Priming your child for what is to come is as simple as keeping them involved and informed.

Talking with your child about going to Kindergarten is a simple way to begin with their preparation. Talk to them about where they are going and what you think they will be able to do, learn and play with at Kindergarten. Discuss with them things such as making friends and trying new things and invite them to share with you what they think it will be like to make new friends and learn new things.

Ask your child to share with you what interests them and what they would like to learn at Kindergarten. This is a great way to find out what they already know and what interests them, and it is relevant information that you can share with your child's Kindergarten Teacher.

Making the transition to Kindergarten familiar and predictable helps your child familiarise themselves with the concept and predict what will happen next.

Discussing with your child about Kindergarten and asking them what they think they will do there is an important step in preparing your child for Kindergarten. It helps them to be able to bring their ideas out of their head and share them to make more sense of them.

If your child is non-verbal or has limited language, you can still do this through your own use of language and interpreting their response. In this situation, you may want to include images such as photos of the Kindergarten or Google images of children playing with different experiences at Kindergarten and use these when discussing with your child. Look for non-verbal responses such as intense scrutinisation of pictures, sounds of excitement, and even withdrawal, which all can inform how your child feels about the images and what you have said. Remember, if your child is non-verbal or has limited language, keep your language short, to between two and five words maximum at a time when talking with your child and give them time to consider and understand what you have said, before moving onto your next question or statement.

Through preparation, you can minimise, and in some cases eliminate, children's separation anxiety. Understand that all children will experience some degree of anxiety about being separated from their parents or primary caregivers, just as some adults experience anxiety when faced with a new challenge or experience. Through diligent planning, we can assist children in changing their separation anxiety or nerves into excitement for the opportunities that are possible.

Making Kindergarten a predictable part of your child's life helps them navigate their world, as they know what will happen in advance.

Practice Runs Make it Fun

As most children in Australia are preparing for Kindergarten during the Christmas holidays, this is a fantastic opportunity for the family to continue the preparation by practising some of the things your child will need to do when they start Kindergarten.

Setting a positive sleep schedule is one of the first and most important things. Work out what time you will need to be at Kindergarten and how long your child needs to get ready in the morning. Then, plan the time your child needs to get up in the morning and use this to calculate the time they need to go to bed. For more information, see the chapter: *Cultivating Restful Sleep Habits*.

Once the sleep routine is in place, next you can begin with a couple of practise drives or walks to Kindergarten, depending on your specific circumstances. It is a good idea to do this at least a couple of times to, one, understand the time you need for travel, two, to help your child understand the process, and three, to help your child become familiar with the Kindergarten.

The practise run can become a fun way for you and your child to experience the Kindergarten before they begin.

Essential Kindergarten Supplies for Success

One piece of advice I give parents before their child starts Kindergarten is to take their child with them to the shop to buy their Kindergarten supplies. Not only do children find it fun to choose their bag or lunch box, but this is also an opportunity to support their development of autonomy.

When selecting different items that your child will need for Kindergarten, it is important to make sure that it is child friendly for your child. That your child can independently open and close their bag, lunch box and drink bottle, or require little help to do so.

When you take your child to buy their Kindergarten supplies, let them have a little play with them. Allow them to play with the zip on the bag, and the latches on the lunch box. Ask them to open the drink bottle. If they can do this themselves, or with little support, then it is a good choice for your child. However, if your child cannot do it and requires you to open it, then it may be better to try a different one.

Once you have narrowed down the things that your child can open independently or with little support, it is ok to give them two or three to choose from. If your child finds it difficult to make decisions, keep it to a choice of two, however if they can handle decision making, then it is okay to give them more to choose from.

Playtime: Fun Ways to Prepare for Kindergarten

Once you have bought all your child's new supplies for Kindergarten, it is time to let them have a little play at home.

Invite your child to help you make their snack and lunch during the holidays. Fill their lunch box and water bottle and allow them to use them at least a few times in the weeks before Kindergarten commences.

Encouraging your child to practice using their lunch box and drink bottle helps them become familiar with how they work, including the pressure needed to open and close them. This also teaches them valuable skills in caring for their belongings.

If you are going out, have your child help pack their Kindergarten bag with their lunch box and drink bottle and practise carrying it on their back. This allows them to get used to using the zip or latches on the bag, as well as getting used to the weight of the bag on their back, which has more benefits, than just independence. According to Play Move Improve, carrying a bag on their back helps to stabilise children's shoulders, develop their core strength and dynamic balance. It has much more benefits than just developing independence.

It is also important to allow your child to get used to wearing the clothes you want them to wear to Kindergarten. Support and encourage your child to practise dressing and undressing in the clothes and shoes they will wear to Kindergarten.

I have often seen children wearing brand-new shoes to Kindergarten, only for them to start saying that they are hurting their feet. Allowing your child to wear the clothes and shoes you intend to send them to Kindergarten in helps your child to get used to them, as well as breaks them in. This is particularly important for shoes, as new shoes that are not worn in can lead to blisters on the feet.

Creating Comfort and Excitement for a Smooth Transition

Preparing your child for Kindergarten begins with making the idea of it feel familiar and exciting. It is about helping your child feel comfortable and excited about Kindergarten. Talking about Kindergarten can ease any fears or uncertainties by replacing the unknown with positive expectations. Share stories about the fun activities they might do, the new friends they can make, and the exciting things they'll learn. Use an enthusiastic tone to build anticipation, showing your child that Kindergarten is an adventure to look forward to. Ask open-ended questions like, "What do you think Kindergarten will be like?" or "What would you like your Teacher to know about you?" These conversations can replace uncertainty with excitement and give you insights into their feelings.

Encourage your child to express their thoughts and feelings creatively by drawing or writing about what they're looking forward to. This can turn worries into actionable ideas while reinforcing their confidence. By framing Kindergarten as an exciting adventure, you can ease their transition and help them approach this new experience with joy and curiosity.

Note: it is good to know what children want to learn, because this can give you opportunities to teach them things you want them to learn, by using what they want to learn as a guide and building other things around that topic or interest.

Simple Strategies for Everyday Learning

Many parents come to Kindergarten expecting a formal program that teaches Literacy and Numeracy. Though we do incorporate these skills into our programs, we do so in a play-based manner, introducing the children to these concepts while they are playing.

Conversations, pictures, and books all support the grasping of Literacy and Numeracy. By exposing children to these concepts in everyday life, we help them to begin to make sense of them.

Parents can incorporate literacy and numeracy at home in several ways. One method is as simple as reading books with their children and asking them what the story is about, and the other is as complex as asking their child to get two apples for a snack.

Involving your child in cooking or shopping helps them learn to count, as well as introduces them to the literacy that is all around them.

Using numeracy language can also be as simple as saying "come here" and "go there."

Through using mathematical language at home, you are exposing your child to the concepts in mathematics, whilst at the same time supporting their literacy skills through learning new words and their uses.

Taking Care of Yourself for a Smoother Transition

After all the work you have done supporting your child's preparation for Kindergarten, parents must also prepare themselves. This is particularly important for parents who have been their child's primary caregiver and have not been separated.

Organise time for you to do things for you whilst your child is at Kindergarten, go for a coffee with friends, see that movie you have been anticipating seeing, find a job that fits in with your schedule. It does not matter how you decide to fill this time, just make sure you plan what you are going to do, so that you can make the most of this brief time and you can avoid worrying about your child.

Key Milestones and How to Support Your Child

Things children do when they are ready to start Kindergarten and what you can do to support them:
- Communication Skills:
  - Able to verbalise their needs in words and/or short sentences.
  - Enjoy talking with adults and/or peers.
  - Have a large vocabulary.
  - Using three and four-word sentences.
  - Able to ask for help.
- Supporting Actions:
  - Repeat back what your child says, expanding to a few extra words.
  - Acknowledge your child's attempts at communication.
  - Tell stories, engage in conversations, and use open-ended questions.

- Speak regularly, read stories, and acknowledge what your child says.
- Encourage children to express themselves when they need assistance.
- Independence and Self-Care:
    - Carry their own bag, which will also support their core strength and motor development.
    - Know what belongs to them.
    - With support, am able to separate from parents and find comfort in trusted adults.
    - Developing resilience. Able to settle, with support, when distressed.
    - Becoming increasingly independent and wanting to do things themselves.
- Supporting Actions:
    - Encourage your child to carry a light bag and gradually increase weight.
    - Involve them in packing their belongings and identifying what is theirs.
    - Practise short separations to build confidence and trust.
    - Acknowledge emotions, offer comfort, and use language to articulate feelings.
    - Praise efforts and encourage self-reliance in small tasks.
- Emotional and Social Development:
    - Developing their emotional intelligence (knowing basic emotions).
    - Know and respond to their name, may know their age as well.
    - Beginning to show interest in socialising with peers.
    - Are aware of the groups they belong to (family, culture, community).

- Beginning to share experiences with others.
- Are becoming aware of fairness and bias.
- Supporting Actions:
  - Talk about emotions in stories and daily situations.
  - Use their name regularly and prompt them to introduce themselves.
  - Arrange playdates, attend playgroups, and encourage social activities.
  - Discuss family, culture, and community involvement.
  - Show interest in their stories and encourage sharing of experiences.
  - Empathise and discuss fairness and bias to nurture understanding.
- Motor Skills and Physical Development:
  - Becoming more confident with gross motor skills (running, climbing).
  - Able to feed themselves with minimal spillage.
  - Able to drink out of a bottle or cup with minimal spillage.
  - Either toilet training or using the toilet.
  - Aware of physical needs like hunger, thirst, rest.
- Supporting Actions:
  - Encourage outside play and activities like climbing, riding, and obstacle courses.
  - Allow self-feeding with appropriate utensils and expectations for accidents.
  - Gradually transition from bottle to cup, modelling cleaning up after spills.
  - Support toilet training with reminders and praise efforts.
  - Notice physical cues for hunger and rest, and prompt appropriately.

- Cognitive Skills and Learning Readiness:
    - Able to follow one and two-step instructions.
    - Beginning to show interest in numbers and letters.
    - Developing a love of stories.
- Supporting Actions:
    - Break down instructions and practise until they can follow independently.
    - Read regularly and talk about numbers and letters in everyday settings.
    - Foster a love for stories by reading, discussing, and storytelling.
- Curiosity and Engagement in Learning:
    - Are curious and enthusiastic to learn new things.
    - Can easily enter play and move to new experiences.
    - Have diverse interests; not fixated on one thing.
- Supporting Actions:
    - Engage in conversations about their interests and explore topics together.
    - Encourage play transitions and demonstrate different play options.
    - Introduce a variety of activities to nurture a balanced range of interests.

Conclusion

Preparation is the key. With good preparation, all children can transition effectively to Kindergarten and have a positive experience. The small things you do to help your child prepare, will have big returns in the enjoyment and positive experience you and your child have at Kindergarten. Enjoy preparing your child for the transition to Kindergarten.

Kindergarten – New Beginnings

Introduction

Starting Kindergarten can be daunting for both children and their parents. It is common for both to have mixed feelings, and this is more evident when the first child is starting Kindergarten.

Understand that you are entering a new experience and that your feelings are valid and that your child's Kindergarten Teacher is here to support your child and you.

In this chapter, you will discover what to expect and how you can navigate challenges that arise.

Preparing for Your Child's Transition

Understanding what to expect when your child begins Kindergarten is key to a smooth transition. Anticipating how children may respond to starting Kindergarten can help parents prepare for any challenges that may arise as their child adjusts. By familiarising themselves with typical reactions, parents can observe their own child's behaviour and create plans that align with their child's unique needs and feelings about being left at Kindergarten.

Knowing what is expected of you before you leave your child at Kindergarten, also makes it easier for you to plan. From signing your child in, supplying any required medication, and having Confidential Information up to date are just a few things parents need to be aware of.

I hope that this will give you some ideas about how to support your child when you leave them at Kindergarten and what is expected of you as a parent.

Navigating the Emotional Journey

When children start Kindergarten, they often fall into two groups. Those who separate easily from their parents and dive straight into the Kindergarten program, or those who cling to their parents, requiring the support of a teacher to help them separate and calm themselves. Though these are the common themes around separation, as children are unique, they will often fall somewhere upon this continuum. Some will require support to separate, but then once the separation is complete, they will self-settle. Others will separate independently, and then something will remind them that their parents are not with them and will require assistance to settle themself.

Walking the Familiar Path

Sometimes parents notice that their child, who at first separated from them and embraced Kindergarten, all of a sudden do not like Kindergarten or require assistance to separate and settle at Kindergarten. I like to think that this is because the novelty of Kindergarten has worn off, and they realise they have to stay there when they want to stay with their parents.

Another possibility I have considered in the past, usually after the child has settled into Kindergarten for a few months, is that the child has matured and suddenly realises that their parents are not there and becomes anxious about whether they will come back.

Whether your child has difficulty at first with separating or this comes later, the chapter: *Separation Made Smoother* will give you more support on how to manage this concern.

Cultivating Growing Independence

As children become more comfortable in Kindergarten, parents may begin to see an increase in their independence at home. This is a good thing, and parents can support their children by giving them small things they can do at home to develop their sense of self-worth and independence.

This can be anything from letting them dress themselves or carry their bag, to helping you to do the shopping or cooking meals. Whenever you allow your child to do something, they are developing their skills, independence, and confidence.

Your child will want to do more and more things themselves, and this can sometimes cause frustration for parents when they are in a hurry and their child insists on dressing themselves or putting on their own shoes. To manage this, parents can add extra time before they expect to leave to allow their child to do these things themselves. It is all about planning and making time work around your child.

However, at times, this may not be possible. In these situations, do not feel bad if you must step in to help your child so you can move on in time. You will not be able to let your child do everything themselves, and this is okay. As long as you allow enough opportunities, your child will eventually understand that sometimes it is okay to ask for or receive help when they cannot do something or run out of time.

Cultivating Positive Behaviours

Teachers and even many parents notice changes in a child's behaviour from time to time. This is understandable, as children are learning about who they are and the world around them. In a Kindergarten setting, children have both new adults and other children to learn from.

When children receive a response to a new behaviour that gives them attention, or when they see another child receive attention for a given behaviour, children will often begin to act in a way that elicits the same or desired response.

This is why you will sometimes see a child who has never engaged in a certain behaviour begin acting in a new way. They have either seen someone, a child or an adult, acting in a specific way and received a desired response, or they themselves have received a desired response from a certain action.

Children learn naturally by mimicking and copying the behaviour of others, observing the consequences of their actions, and experimenting with their own behaviours to see what responses they elicit.

If the behaviour is undesirable, the best response is to not give the behaviour any attention. Instead, focus your attention on the behaviour you find desirable and encourage this by responding to this behaviour favourably.

As with anything that is challenging or of concern, if this does not work, speak to your child's Teacher, Maternal Health Nurse or Doctor about possible solutions or referral pathways to help with managing these behaviours. You will learn more in the chapter: *Nurturing Positive Behaviour.*

Essential Insights for Parents

There are many things parents need to know when their child is going to start Kindergarten.

There is a lot of legal paperwork that is necessary such as Child Confidential Records, Immunisation History Statement declarations, discussions around additional needs and more.

Child Confidential Records

These are important legal documents that contain all the information about your child. The information collected here helps the Teacher understand who your child is and what support they may need. This will include their name and date of birth, as well as emergency contacts, allergies, and additional needs. It is important to ensure that all the information is accurate and up to date so that the Teaching staff can support your child in the best way possible for their specific needs.

It is important that the information in this document is up to date. For example, if circumstances change and you need to add or remove an emergency contact, you must notify your child's Teacher as soon as possible so they can make the necessary adjustments. This document specifies, among other things, who the child is allowed to be released to, so it is essential that it is accurate and up to date.

Immunisation History Statement

In Victoria, Australia, the government has a No Jab, No Play policy. This means that every child starting Kindergarten must be up to date with their Immunisation. This is a means to prevent childhood illnesses that are preventable by vaccinations.

If you do not know if your child is up to date with their Immunisations, please speak to your child's Teacher so they can help you to understand how to gain a copy of their Immunisation History Statement. This can be done through Medicare either online, via the app, telephone call, or in person.

If you have any concerns, speak to your child's Teacher, Maternal Health Nurse or Doctor for further information and possible solutions.

Additional Needs

It is important to inform your child's teacher if your child has any additional needs. This helps the Teacher to make informed decisions about how to support your child at Kindergarten.

It is important that the teacher knows whether the additional needs are physical, medical, or learning. This information will help them prepare a Kindergarten Inclusion Support (KIS) application.

The KIS funding can offer extra support to your child and the Kindergarten as a whole through:

- Funding for capitol works such as ramps or visibility materials.
- Funding for Additional Assistants to increase the Child to Staff ratio (Note that the Additional Assistant is there to support the whole program, not just your child. They enable one of the staff to supply the one-to-one support your child may need)
- Funding for mentoring and or training, including medical needs training like peg feeding.
- Funding for Mentoring and Program development support

It is crucial that this information is shared with your child's teacher, even if you do not think your child requires the support.

In one Kindergarten I had a parent come through the enhanced Maternal Health Nurse who had a child with Downs Syndrome. When the Preschool Field Officer and I were speaking to them, we brought up the topic of applying for KIS funding. Initially, the parent was not interested, they did not want their child to be treated differently to the other children. I explained that the funding not only helps us to be able to support their child, but it also enables us to keep the same level of support for all of the other children.

When the parents returned the next week, they told us they had considered what we had told them and how it would help all the children. They then agreed to our application and the support we could provide their child.

Signing in at Kindergarten

Regardless of what method your child's Kindergarten uses, they will have something that you need to sign your child in when you drop them off at Kindergarten. It is essential that you are aware of how this process works.

I have worked with written systems where parents had to write the time, the name of who was collecting and their signature, as well as a digital system that required the parents to use their login details, and it recorded the time for them.

If you are uncertain about the process, please speak to your child's Teacher and ask them to clarify it for you or even help you with it.

Kindergarten – New Beginnings

The same goes for signing your child out at the end of the day.

Please ensure you know the operating hours of your child's Kindergarten session and that you plan enough time to collect your child on time. Not only can it be stressful for your child if you are late, but this also impacts on your child's teacher's ability to do their administrative duties, in particular impacting on the ability to join meetings or liaise with parents or other stakeholders.

Communication is the Key

Effective, open, and honest communication between yourself and your child's Kindergarten Teacher is key to building positive relationships and ensuring that your child receives the appropriate support.

Whenever your child's situation changes, whether physical, health-related, or emotional, it is important to share this with the Kindergarten Teacher. This applies whether the dynamics at home change or you add or remove people from the authorised contacts for your child.

If you have difficulties communicating with them, either due to a language barrier or just not understanding, it is important to get someone to help get this message to your child's Kindergarten Teacher so they can make necessary adjustments to how they communicate, such as accessing translator services or finding a means of communication that helps you to understand.

Conclusion

By being aware of how your child may react when left at Kindergarten and of your responsibilities, you can approach the Kindergarten experience in a positive way, armed with strategies and knowing you are not alone.

You can also minimise or even eliminate any anxiety or apprehension your child may feel about starting or attending Kindergarten.

Working with your child's Kindergarten Teacher to establish an effective communication plan between you and them is the best thing you can do to support your child both at Kindergarten and beyond.

Separation Made Smoother

Introduction

Separation anxiety is something that many children experience at one time or another. It is a natural part of the process of children transitioning from the familiarity of the family, to the unfamiliar of a Kindergarten setting and beyond.

How parents and teachers address this will determine how well a child is able to transition to and embrace the wonder that is Kindergarten.

Why Validating Feelings Matters

Ignoring your child's feelings about going to Kindergarten will make the experience challenging, to say the least. Brushing off how your child is feeling only teaches them that their feelings are not important and that expressing how you feel is a negative thing to do. Both of these are incorrect, but in a child's eyes, this is what they learn to believe.

We will learn more about teaching children about emotional intelligence in the chapter: *Empowering Emotional Intelligence.*

Trauma and Transition: The Rise of Anxiety in Children Post-COVID-19

In 2023, according to Monash Health Allied Health practitioners who have supported the Kindergartens that I have worked at in Melbourne's Southeast, the prevalence of separation anxiety and mental health concerns has increased dramatically since the COVID-19 Pandemic. We all know the stress that the lockdowns and uncertainty created in adults.

Adults have well-developed coping skills compared to children. Acknowledging the ongoing trauma of young children who spent their first few years of life, in a highly stressed world, enables you, as a parent to give the appropriate support necessary to ensure your child is able to manage the challenges that life will often give them.

Viewing children, who were born or lived through the COVID-19 Pandemic, as having lived through trauma encourages you to approach them with greater empathy than if we ignore the challenges they have faced in their short lives. Understanding that your child is not the only one facing these difficulties can give comfort to you and also open up opportunities for you to create supportive relationships with other families who are experiencing the same thing.

Navigating the Separation Journey Together

If your child experiences separation anxiety, speak with them about what will happen at Kindergarten, that you will return, and when.

Most kindergarten children are not fully aware of time. However, letting them know that you will return after lunch, at rest time, or in a time they can recognise will help them begin to build an internal time frame they can draw upon.

Talk with your child's teacher about your child's anxiety and work out a plan that is appropriate for your child. You could sit down and do one activity with them to help them settle in, or you could take them to a specific teacher when it is time for you to go.

When you are ready to leave, kiss and hug your child or perform your own farewell, and then say goodbye and leave immediately. Do not delay the separation once you have begun. This will only add to their anxiety. This is particularly important if they become upset, as they will not be able to settle until they see that you have left.

Remember, their teachers will be right there to support them through these strong emotions.

If you think of pulling a Band-Aid off, you will realize that it hurts a lot more if you pull it off slowly than if you pull it off quickly. The same is true for children who are separated from their parents. A short farewell routine enables your child to deal with the emotions of the separation, process and manage these feelings with the support of trusted adults, and recover, enabling them to engage in their Kindergarten learning environment.

I learnt from a psychologist from Monash Health Allied Health through our school readiness funding, that children who are experiencing separation anxiety cannot recover and deal with the feelings until the separation has occurred. When a separation is delayed, this increases the stress created by the anxiety and it continues to grow and compound until the separation has occurred. It is the anticipation of something that creates fear or excitement, not necessarily the event itself. By decreasing the build-up, we enable children to reach the recovery point sooner and they can begin to deal with the feelings and begin to engage in the program.

If we think about wild animals; a gazelle is grazing on the plains. It is calm and at peace. Then, it hears a sound that alerts it that something is close by. Its ears prick, and its heart starts racing. The gazelle turns its head and sees a lion stalking nearby.

Immediately, its fight-or-flight system kicks in. Its heart starts beating faster, and it draws in more breath and tenses to run. The lion launches its attack, and the gazelle takes off, running this way and that, jumping, doing all it can to escape.

After several minutes, the gazelle loses the lion, finds safe ground, takes some deep breaths, and shudders. It then resets itself and resumes grazing, knowing it is safe.

This scenario demonstrates what happens when an animal is put under distress, faces the threat and recovers.

If we consider the lingering goodbye at Kindergarten, it is like a lion making the gazelle run a marathon rather than a sprint. Eventually, the gazelle's energy would falter, and it would fall prey to the lion. This is the same with children when the goodbye is lingering, or when parents keep returning when their child continues to cry.

I understand it is painfully hard for parents to leave their crying child; I understand that as a father, too. Be assured that the Kindergarten teachers are devoted to caring for your child. Your child, like the gazelle, will face this obstacle, recover, and be able to engage in their learning environment.

Preparation for a Calm Transition

As discussed earlier, preparation is the key to positive transitions. It is also key to decreasing the severity of separation anxiety.

To support your child, you could create a visual weekly calendar, colour-coded for the days your child goes to Kindergarten. Getting your child to help pack their bag and lunchbox also helps to give them some ownership and control in a situation they feel they do not have control.

Talking to your child about the fun things they do at Kindergarten, the friends they play with, and the teachers they like helps build familiarity, which also helps decrease their anxiety.

A note to consider: if your child gets agitated or their anxiety increases, review how you are preparing them. You may be giving them too much to think about and need to pull it back to a level your child is able to cope with. You will know your child best and whether the recommendations I am giving will be effective for them. If this does not work and you still have concerns, speak to your child's Kindergarten Teacher for further support and recommendations.

We want to make Kindergarten feel familiar and safe, not something to fear or worry about.

The Art of Saying Goodbye

As I mentioned earlier, it is important to leave once you say goodbye. I understand that it may be difficult to watch your child crying or screaming as you leave; however, returning to them when this is occurring only reinforces that they are not going to be okay when you leave.

On the other hand, leaving immediately enables your child to deal with how they are feeling and enter the recovery phase, which then allows them to move on and engage in the program.

Your child's teachers will be there to support your child in the way that best serves them. Most children will have at least one staff member they connect well with, whom they will approach to seek help to settle after the separation has occurred.

Rarely will a child be unresponsive to the staff. In these situations, we acknowledge how the child is feeling, and if they do not want support, we leave them to work through their feelings, ensuring that they are always safe. Safety is paramount, and this goes beyond physical safety. We do our best to ensure that your child has the support they need when they need it and remain accessible to your child when they are ready to come to us.

An Initial goodbye routine could be as follows:

- Arrive at Kindergarten and help your child put their bag away.
- As your child washes their hands, you sign them in.
- Sit together either for a story or a puzzle.
- Find a familiar Teacher they feel comfortable with.
- Complete your goodbye ritual (e.g. hug, kiss, hi-5).
- Say goodbye and leave them with their teacher.

Visualising Transitions: The Power of Social Stories

Social stories are a great tool for home use. Gather images of your child in kindergarten, them playing, and pictures of you, put them together in Canva, Publisher, or Word, and print or make a PDF copy to use on a device.

The idea of a Social Story is to create a visual story that you can read with your child. In this instance, the story would ideally include images of the Kindergarten, showing the routine you follow when you arrive, such as putting the child's bag away, washing their hands, signing them in, reading a story, and then saying goodbye.

You can create a Social Story for anything that your child needs support with.

Alternatively, you can speak to your child's teacher and ask them to create one for you. In either situation, it is good to have a copy of the Social Story at Kindergarten for the teachers to read with your child, and a copy at home for you to read.

In my experience, using a Social Story effectively, will within a few weeks help most children transition and separate from their parents in the morning, less if the child attends Kindergarten multiple days a week.

One specific example was of a child who came to visit the Kindergarten with their parent. They were looking for a new service, as they did not feel supported at the service they were attending. The child had a lot of separation anxiety and would struggle to leave their parents at drop-off time.

As the walkthrough was drawing to an end, I excused myself and went and printed off a copy of the Social Story I had made for the children in my group. I gave it to the child and explained to the parent how to use it.

Fast forward a month and the child had started at my Kindergarten. There was lots of separation anxiety as their parent left. The child clung to them for support. Over the coming weeks, the child began to separate easier from their parent. The tears lessened until there were none.

I discussed the story with their parents, who explained that they read it regularly at home. They always read it twice just before leaving for Kindergarten, and because the child was so familiar with it, they were able to tell the story themself.

I was amazed. One day, I was thinking about what to do for group time and I asked the child if they wanted to tell their peers the Social Story, they nodded. I got the service copy of the Social Story, and the child told them, in detail, the Social Story. This occurred near the end of the session and the child continued as parents came in to collect their children. Everyone was amazed with this child.

I must share that this child was in my three-year-old group, and I am so very proud of them and what their parents have done to help them go from severe Separation Anxiety to an active and engaged member of the Kindergarten who easily made friends.

See the special offers section for your free Separation Anxiety Social Story.

When Extra Support is Needed

It is rare that extra support is needed for children with Separation Anxiety. In situations where the support we can offer at Kindergarten is not sufficient, teachers can access the PSFO program (Pre-School-Field Officer). PSFOs are Kindergarten-trained staff who help build teachers' capacity to deliver age-appropriate programs. They can also provide observations and recommendations on individual children and the group as a whole.

Where staff do not have the answer, the PSFO sometimes can support them to bridge the gap that is impacting the child. The PSFO or your child's teacher may also recommend further assessments if they believe that the Separation Anxiety is contributed to by other factors that need specialist support and investigations, such as a paediatrician, speech therapist or occupational therapist. Remember, if this is recommended it is not a reflection on you. It is done in the best interest of your child.

Conclusion

Through preparation and collaboration with your child's teacher, you can create a smooth and successful transition into Kindergarten with little or no separation anxiety. Where separation anxiety persists, there are many things you can do to support your child and make this challenging time rewarding and enjoyable for you and your child.

The Power of Playtime

Introduction

The Victorian early years learning and development framework states: "Play is essential to the health and wellbeing of children. Through play, babies and young children explore their environment, express curiosity, build confidence, and engage in problem-solving, which contributes to a sense of agency and builds on their learning dispositions" (VEYLDF, p. 11). In early childhood education, agency refers to children's ability to make choices, influence events, and have a sense of control over their actions and interactions within their environment. It emphasises respecting children as active participants in their own learning and development, capable of expressing their ideas, preferences, and perspectives.

Children learn best through play. Any research you look up on the benefits of play shows that this is the best format for children to learn. If you do a search in Google Scholar you will see there are over 2.5 million results for the search parameter "benefit of play in children's development".

It is the natural state of a child to play and explore in everything they do. In the words of Maria Montessori, "Play is the work of the child." Allowing children the opportunity to explore and play throughout the day enables them to make sense of the world around them, create neural pathways that are essential for healthy brain development, and creates muscle memory for the physical skills they learn.

Empowering Insights: The Key to Meaningful Learning

Without a foundational understanding of how children learn, we are unlikely to fully understand where they are developmentally and what they need to thrive. We often view a child through the eyes of an adult rather than as an active participant in their learning journey, leading to unrealistic expectations about what they can or cannot achieve. By having a basic understanding of what your child is learning through their play, helps you to gauge where they are developmentally and will help you make more informed decisions when concerns arise.

To start with, sit or kneel down on the floor with your child and look at the world around you. This will help you understand how your child sees the world around them.

The Power of Playtime

What is Play: The Foundation of Learning

Play is an enjoyable experience and a means of making sense of what is happening around us. Children explore the world through play. At first, babies explore the world through their senses. As children grow, they begin to introduce more complex ways of learning through exploration, hypothesising, theorising, experimentation, trial, and error.

Through the various ways children learn, your child will explore and incorporate their understanding of the world around them, including beliefs, social and cultural customs, spirituality and more.

The Foundations of Learning: Key Dispositions for Growth

There are many different learning dispositions that your child will learn through. These include:

- Commitment – the ability to stick to a task until they have achieved their goal.
- Confidence – believing in their own abilities, knowledge, and skills.
- Cooperation – the ability to work with others to achieve a common goal.
- Creativity – representing the world through creative means such as art, music, dance, and movement.
- Curiosity – being curious about the world around them, how and why things are the way they are.
- Enthusiasm – brings energy and enjoyment to the world they live in and the work they are doing.

- Imagination – the ability to represent the world through their own internal dialogue visually, verbally, or physically.
- Persistence – the ability to continue in the face of obstacles and challenges.
- Reflexivity – becoming aware of the ways their experiences, interests, and beliefs shape their understanding.

Learning Styles Unpacked: A Guide for Parents

There are many styles of learning that encompass the different ways children learn. Depending on the source you use, this can range from four to eight different styles of learning. The four learning styles that I focus on are visual, auditory, tactile, and kinaesthetic.

- Visual learners absorb information by observing and interpreting their surroundings, making sense of what they see.
- Auditory learners process information through hearing, which may involve listening to stories or audiobooks, following spoken instructions, singing songs, or even speaking aloud.
- Tactile learners thrive through hands-on experiences, such as physical play, sensory activities, manipulating objects, writing, and creative arts.
- Kinaesthetic learners excel by engaging their bodies to move and explore through activities like climbing, running, jumping, and dancing.

No one learning style is better than the other. Over time, children will learn all the learning styles. However, in the beginning, they will process the world through the learning style that suits them best. As they gain more experience using these styles, they will slowly adapt and include them.

This is why children often gravitate toward and repeat certain experiences, such as painting, digging in the sand pit, or running.

Building your child's learning opportunities around their primary learning style, will help them to make sense of the world, as well as support in strengthening the other learning styles. This is a strength-based approach.

When we focus on a weakness, we can improve it a little bit. However, when we focus on a strength, we not only strengthen this but also improve other areas on which we are not directly focusing. That is why a strength-based approach is preferable in any situation.

Unveiling the Learning Journey: What Children Gain Through Play

It can be overwhelming for parents when a teacher explains everything their child is learning through the various types of play they engage with. Below is an exhaustive list of the different things children learn from a range of play experiences. You can read the whole list, or you can jump straight to the ones that your child prefers to engage with.

Drawing

When children draw and colour in pictures, they are learning a variety of skills. They learn and develop their fine motor skills, particularly their fine muscle strength and control which are necessary for later developing a tripod grip. They also learn shape and form, dimensions, and interpretation of thought and colours, and develop their imagination through creating images based upon their thoughts. Children learn to express themselves through the images they create, as well as developing their communication skills when they share what they have drawn with others. In addition to this, children develop their core strength which is important in all areas of their life.

Painting
Painting offers similar learning opportunities to drawing. Colour mixing is an advantage of painting over drawing. Children will also learn to control the pressure they use when painting, as too much pressure will tear the paper. With its layering possibilities, painting offers a greater level of creativity. Finger painting also brings in the sensory experience through touch, including temperature, texture, and moistness.

Collage
Collage offers opportunities for a greater level of complex skills, including material selection (decision making), cutting, positioning, pasting, using sticky tape dispensers, and their imagination. For some children, the process of pasting a cotton wool ball on a piece of paper can be a great achievement, whilst, for other children, it is creating a complex collage. Children often combine collage and drawing or painting to take their art to a completely different level.

Playdough and clay
Playing with playdough and clay helps children further develop their fine motor grip through various methods, such as pinching, pulling, gripping, rolling, and utilizing specialist tools. They also learn through the sensory feedback of pressure, texture, temperature, etc. This can be a soothing experience for children

who have sensory processing difficulties or difficulties managing their emotions.

Sensory play

Sensory play, including goop, slime, sand, and mud, enables children to develop their sensory feedback understanding. It also can include some experimentation (science concepts) when children are involved in the creation of the sensory material. Sensory play can be calming to many children.

Sand pit and dirt play

These areas utilise some of the sensory play skills as mentioned before. They also incorporate gross motor skills, through digging, raking, pouring etc. Sand and dirt play can be messy, giving lots of sensory feedback. In Kindergarten, these are high traffic areas, which also give children the opportunity to practice collaboration and negotiation with their peers.

Gross motor play

Gross motor play enables children to develop their large muscle control and confidence in risk-taking. Learning to climb an A-frame or other climbing equipment includes gross motor control, hand-eye coordination, calculated risk-taking, body awareness, and spatial awareness. Learning to move over the top of an A-frame or similar object takes skill and time, particularly learning to turn the body at the apex and climb down the other side backwards. Gross motor also includes other movement, including running, skipping, and jumping. Most children learn best when they have opportunities to move, whether that be big or small movement.

Jumping

Children love to jump, including onto a crash mat. Have you ever heard your child say, "Look how high I can jump," and then demonstrate for you? Jumping incorporates body awareness, spatial awareness, and calculated risk-taking. It also includes safety awareness, i.e., not jumping when peers or objects are in the landing area.

Bikes, scooters, and stair walking

Bike riding, scooter riding, and walking on stairs offer different means of practising body movement and spatial awareness. They incorporate a greater focus on balance and core strength to maintain a balanced position. This focus extends to other modes of transport children may use, including caterpillar walkers.

Block construction

Through block construction, children learn about shapes, size, position, and balance whilst demonstrating their creativity and imagination through constructing scenes with blocks. Larger blocks require more gross motor involvement, where small blocks require more fine motor involvement.

Dressing up and dramatic play

Through dressing up, children are able to explore a variety of personalities and identities. They learn to take on the role of the characters they are portraying. They may act out the role of a police officer or a nurse, a mum or dad, and they may even become a superhero and help people. This also often incorporates many language skills as children act out their role, telling peers who they are and what they are doing.

Pretend play

Pretend play supports children to take real world experiences and enact them through a micro world, through the use of toys and props. This is particularly useful for children who are experiencing trauma, as they can work through their feelings through the toys and props they are using and separate it from themselves. This encourages the development of their language skills, imagination, and emotional regulation.

Reading and writing

Children are developing their literacy and language skills all the time, whilst they are listening to adults and peers communicate, listening to stories and telling stories. This even begins whilst your child is in utero. As soon as the ears are formed, they are learning language. More directly, in reading and listening to stories, children are also learning about grammar, pronunciation, vocabulary, the correct way to hold a book and the direction of reading and writing.

Writing

Children develop their fine motor skills through writing. They also begin to discover the direction of writing, letter shapes, and word forms. They begin to commit to memory familiar words, such as their name and names of familiar others, and learn to be able to recreate these in their own writing. For children to be competent and confident with writing, they need to develop their fine motor skills, along with their understanding of the written word. They also need to develop good core strength to enable them to sit appropriately to write. Children must learn to do scribble and scratching first before they are able to start to create the complex shapes and combinations that make up writing.

Music and movement

Music and movement enable children to learn to be able to follow rhymes and rhythms, increase vocabulary, and develop motor control and core strength. They improve memory, through repeating songs that they are familiar with and improve their vocabulary and pronunciation of words. Movement also enables children to develop their spatial awareness, through dance and actions.

Puzzles

Puzzles help children develop problem-solving skills, fine motor skills, decision-making, and hypothesising. They help them look for similar objects, either in shape or colour, and match the corresponding pieces to the correct place.

Matching games

Matching games help children recognise patterns and determine similarities between objects. This is an essential skill for future literacy, numeracy, and mathematical concepts. Matching games are a different way of supporting children in developing their problem-solving skills.

Numbers

There are many opportunities to incorporate numbers and numeracy skills in Kindergarten. These range from simple activities requiring children to draw a specific number of dots to coincide with a number in an activity, to children using mathematical language such as here, there, near, far, big, and small. Children also participate in counting at various times, either during head counts or as part of songs or games.

Communication

Communication is a core discipline of a Kindergarten program. Communication is used all the time when welcoming children and families, giving directions and discussing what the children are doing. A rich language environment will also incorporate a variety of languages, either the children's home languages or the staff using home languages. When children or staff have a first language other than English, it is encouraged that they use these at Kindergarten, along with English. It is important that if a child has a first language that is not English, the child should be exposed to their first or mother tongue as much as possible, particularly using it at home and with their family. Children pick up a second language much easier, when they are proficient in their first language. Supporting the development of a child's first language also assists them to understand the use of grammar in both their first language and in English.

Experiments and science

Experiments are a great way for children to develop their literacy and numeracy skills. They develop their language skills through listening to directions, asking questions and making observations and comments about the experiment and the process. They develop their numeracy skills through learning how much of different ingredients are required, as well as the language of measurements. Science also encourages children to make hypotheses about what they expect to happen and encourages them to make modifications to an experiment to see what results they might get.

Self-help skills

Self helps skills such as dressing, toileting, resting, and eating help children to learn to regulate their own bodies. They learn to understand when their body is giving them a sign that they need one of the above. It also helps to develop self-esteem and confidence as a child learns to be able to do more things for themselves. Most children begin to assert their independence by the time they have started kindergarten. Simple things like encouraging your child to pack and carry their bags have wide-reaching positive returns for you and your child.

Conclusion

Everything your child does, everywhere, teaches them something. By understanding how children learn through play and exploration, as well as the different types of play and what children learn through them, you can support your child in becoming knowledgeable and the best version of themselves. By keeping your expectations age-appropriate, your child can flourish and become a lifelong learner.

Empowering Emotional Intelligence

Introduction

Several years ago, I read *"Raising Emotionally Intelligent Children"* by John Gottman. I heard about this book through a course I had undertaken and immediately went out and bought it. From this book, I learnt about the importance of teaching children emotional intelligence and being an emotion coach.

Though I was still learning at the time, it made a lot of sense both professionally and personally as a father of three children. After five years I was able to complement this basic understanding through undertaking the "Tuning into Kids®" facilitator training, which I am now a qualified facilitator.

Understanding and supporting children's emotional intelligence is a passion of mine and something I aim to weave into every session I run as a Kindergarten Teacher, and mentor and guide other staff in how to be an emotion coach. Something I am still learning to incorporate.

Why Children Need an Emotion Coach

Young children are learning every second of every day. In fact, as soon as they have self-awareness, they are learning. From the baby in utero who turns towards a familiar voice, newborns learning to communicate their needs through crying, to kindergarten aged children learning to communicate their needs verbally and interact on a social level with those around them.

The same goes for their emotional intelligence. Children need guidance to learn about their emotions and the emotions of others and how to respond appropriately to them.

Ignoring your child's emotional outburst sends a message that their emotions do not matter. This can lead to behavioural and other issues that can create difficulties for your child.

By giving your child time, and acknowledging their emotions, you can help your child develop their emotional intelligence. It has been shown that emotional intelligence is a more accurate indicator of a child's potential than their IQ.

What is emotional Intelligence?

According to Lauren Landry's blog on Harvard Business School online, "Emotional Intelligence in Leadership: Why It's Important", the core competencies of emotional intelligence are:

1. Self-awareness
2. Self-management
3. Social awareness
4. Relationship management

When you consider these skills through a parent's perspective on your child's development, you will see them as follows:

1. Self-awareness – recognising their own emotions and being able to name and explain how they feel.
2. Self-management – ability to self-regulate their own emotions and behaviour in the face of their emotions.
3. Social awareness – ability to recognise the emotions and feelings of others and be able to name and explain them.
4. Relationship management – able to use this information to successfully engage in relationships with others.

Emotional intelligence is the learned knowledge of emotions, both within oneself and in those around one. It includes the ability to name and explain these emotions and how they feel, as well as the knowledge of how to use this information to establish relationships and respond appropriately to these emotions in others.

Cultivating Emotional Vocabulary

An easy step to start with, is to begin bringing in a diversity of emotional language. Expand the types of emotions you use when you are talking to your child. Most young children recognise about four emotions, which usually are the following:

1. Happy
2. Sad
3. Angry
4. Scared

When your child is using these words to describe how they are feeling, expand their understanding by adding in other words. For instance, if your child says, "I am very happy," you could say, "Oh, are you feeling ecstatic?" Alternatively, if your child says, "I am very sad," you could say, "You look miserable." Not only are you acknowledging what your child is feeling, you are also building upon their emotional vocabulary which will help to develop their emotional intelligence.

One-on-One: The Key to Effective Emotion Coaching

When you decide to take the opportunity to be your child's emotion coach, there is one important rule. Emotion coaching is something you do one-on-one with your child. If you have more than one child, please do not attempt to do the coaching in the presence of other children.

A key factor in emotion coaching is intimacy, which cannot be achieved if there is more than one child. You need to be able to give the child you are coaching all of your attention.

Empowering Emotional Intelligence

When I was undertaking the facilitator training for 'Tuning into Kids®,' they said that if 30% of your time spent with your child is dedicated to emotion coaching, they will receive the benefit. It is not necessary to do it all the time, and the more attuned to their emotions your child becomes, the less time you will need to be their emotion coach.

The time you dedicate to helping your child develop emotional intelligence may seem like a lot at first, but you will soon realise that it is actually a more efficient use of your and their time.

An example was given in a script that the participants had to roleplay a scenario of a child not wanting to put their shoes on to leave in the morning, because they did not want to go to Kindergarten or somewhere else. The parent tries to rationalise why they have to get ready and became frustrated whilst the child becomes more vocal and argumentative. Eventually in this example the parent gives into their child and stays home or gets angry and drags them out to the car. Both scenarios are not effective and appropriate ways to handle the situation.

The emotion coaching example took more time on paper, but in reflecting, the participants could see how acknowledging how the child felt and talking about it, while helping to put their shoes on, helped the parent understand why the child was objecting. Understanding the why behind a child's emotions gives a parent so much more insight into what is going on inside of them and what may be causing them to behave or react in a certain way.

Five Essential Steps for Emotion Coaching

In emotion coaching there are five steps to successfully coach your child through handling their emotions.

Emotion coaching can be done in the same way as a sports coach who breaks down a skill into its components.

Before I share the five steps, consider the last time one of your friends experienced an emotional experience and how you helped them manage it. The trainers of Tuning into Kids® say that most adults are effective at coaching their friends through their emotions but forget how to do this with their children.

Tuning into Kids® describe the five steps of Emotion Coaching as:

1. Become aware of their emotion, especially at lower intensity.
2. View their emotion as an opportunity for connection and teaching.
3. Communicate your understanding and acceptance of the emotion.
4. Help them use words to describe how they feel.
5. If necessary, help them to solve problems. You may also communicate that all wishes and feelings are acceptable, but some behaviours are not.

To make it easier to remember, I have renamed the steps as the ABCDS of Emotion Coaching to help you remember and recall each step. They are based on the steps above and the steps parents will learn through undertaking the Tuning into Kids® program.

Empowering Emotional Intelligence

My five steps of Emotion Coaching are:

1. Awareness
2. Bonding
3. Communication
4. Describing
5. Solving

Awareness

Become aware that an emotion is occurring. The aim is to recognise the lower-level or lower-intensity emotions so that you can support your child in managing them before they become too intense and overwhelm your child.

Examples of low-intensity emotions are joy, contentment, sadness, boredom, and frustration.

Bonding

View the appearance of the emotion as an opportunity for intimacy between you and your child. Be available for them and show them that you care about them and how they feel.

When you dismiss or disregard your child's feelings or emotions, you are telling them that their emotions and feelings are not important. When you acknowledge them, you are saying that you recognise how they feel, that you care, and that you will help them express and manage their feelings.

Communication

Communicate to your child what you understand about the emotion they are feeling and that you accept they are experiencing this emotion. It is important to communicate that you understand and recognise their emotion. This shows that you are focusing on the emotion and how they are feeling, rather than on their behaviour. It also builds on the intimacy in the previous step.

Note

Before I continue with the last two steps, there is an important point to mention here. When your child is experiencing a higher intensity emotion such as anger, rage, or fear, you may only be able to do the first three steps and hold space for your child whilst they coregulate with you. When they are calm again, allow them to move on to whatever is next in their routine. It is not necessary to return immediately and go into step four and five, as this may retrigger your child's emotional response.

You can wait until later in the day, when your child is calm and has been able to process the emotion they experienced, before proceeding to the last two steps. Alternatively, you may choose to wait and talk to your child the next day, after they have had a good sleep, about the emotion they experienced, how it felt, and what they could do next time.

Describing

Help your child to describe in words, action, or assisted technology how the emotion felt in their body and where it was situated. This may be interesting to you, as not everyone experiences emotions the same way. Having experienced anxiety, which is associated with the emotion of fear, for most of my life, I have always felt it as an uneasiness in the stomach, and when it gets extremely high, a creeping feeling that seems to go up my back and across my shoulders. Other people feel it in the chest area as tightness and a rapid heartbeat. Neither is wrong, it is just how different individuals feel the emotion.

This is a good time to introduce other words. For instance, if your child says, "I was really scared," you could say, "You were frightened." The words mean the same; however, "frightened" has a higher intensity.

Remember to remain intimate right through the whole debrief and emotion coaching session you are doing with your child. This will help them to feel more comfortable communicating their emotions and how they feel and gradually decrease the intensity over time.

Solving

This is where problem-solving comes in. In an older child, all you might need to say is, "What could you do next time?" and this may prompt them to produce their own ideas. However, with a younger child, or a child who either has a speech or other delay, this is a time for you to teach some strategies more explicitly.

For instance, you may suggest that your child could next time find a quiet place to sit down, close their eyes and take some deep, belly-breathing breaths, to help them to calm down. Alternatively, your child may say that they were very restless and had too much energy. You could go through the previous steps acknowledging their emotion and extending by introducing the word agitated and then ask, "What could you do to use your energy?" Your child may say, "I can go out the back and run around." Alternatively, you could work with your child to create alternatives if they cannot think of what they could do, such as, "We need holes dug in the veggies patch," or "You could climb up the big tree." Younger children and children with additional needs may require more support to problem solve, whereas an older child may only need you to make a suggestion to prompt them to formulate their own ideas on how to manage their emotions.

Applying Emotion Coaching: Real-Life Examples

After doing my facilitator training, I was excited about my newfound knowledge and eager to share it with colleagues and families. The first day I was working with the children after the training, was the first time I was able to put my new knowledge and skills into practice.

It was the end of the session, and we had a variety of toys out for the children to play with, whilst they waited for their parents to come and collect them.

For the purpose of the following example, I have given some children different names so to maintain their anonymity and for confidentiality.

Murry joined Mary, who was building with magnetic shapes. Murry had additional needs, and it was a joy to watch him join in and play with another child. Mary's parents arrived, she finished building, and left, leaving Murry to continue building. He was intensely focused on what he was making. The tower was almost one metre tall.

Empowering Emotional Intelligence

As Murry put a piece on the top, the tower crumbled and collapsed down into a pile. He stood there for a moment, then all of a sudden, he bolted across the room, threw himself onto the seat of the teacher's chair face first and then crumbled onto the floor crying.

Murry was inconsolable, and in the past, I would have approached and said something like, "It's okay. Mummy will be here soon," which would have dismissed his feeling by thinking I was redirecting or distracting him. Now I know better, and I did better on the day.

I knelt next to Murry, put my hand on his back and said, "It's so frustrating when you are making something, and it breaks. It's okay to be upset." Then I just sat with him.

A minute or so later Murry got up and came to me for a hug, which he had never done before. I just hugged him until he was ready to let go.

Compared to other times when he had become distressed with something, Murry calmed down so much quicker than when I had previously attempted to support him.

Another time, Janis was distressed when his parents left. His Occupational Therapist came to visit, and seeing that he was upset, the Therapist said, "Janis, you're okay. Let's go play outside." This struck me, as I honestly thought the Occupational Therapist would have had more awareness or training in helping children manage emotions.

Witnessing this, I walked over and modelled some emotion coaching without naming it. I knelt down in front of Janis, put my arms out, and said, "Do you want a hug?" They dove straight in. Then I said, "It's hard to say goodbye to Dad. He will come back, and we will keep you safe until he does." After a minute, he let go and then calmly went with his Occupational Therapist to play outside.

I had a further example of this while the children were playing outside on the same day. Nicholas fell over and was upset. Then, another child's Occupational Therapist walked over and said, "You're okay."

I was already heading over to Nicholas when I heard this. Immediately, I knelt down again and said, "Do you need a hug?" Nicholas (who was from another room) came for a hug. Then I acknowledged, "Did you hurt yourself?" They nodded, and I asked them where. I helped them check to make sure there was no blood while acknowledging that it hurt. This helped the child calm down quickly, and they then moved off to continue playing.

The Value of Investing Time in Emotion Coaching

Parents often think that if they pay attention to their child when they are experiencing an emotion, it takes longer than just doing whatever it is for them or getting into an argument with them and making them do what they want them to do.

However, though it takes a little more time in the beginning as you develop the skill, in the long run, Emotion Coaching is a lot more time efficient than dismissing your child's feelings and getting frustrated. Taking the time to develop your ability to Emotion Coach with your child, will make a world of difference for both of your lives.

Empowering Emotional Intelligence

Tuning into Kids® Parenting Program

The Tuning into Kids® Parenting Program is a two-hour by six-week program. Each week builds upon the knowledge gained in the week before. There is a mixture of theory, explanation, and hands-on role-play to help parents to develop the skills they will learn.

The program can be delivered in person, online and in one-on-one situations (this is more a clinical style focussing on specific issues a family faces).

The group size ranges from six to eight participants to ensure that there is enough time for everyone to practice the different roles and skills and receive appropriate feedback.

For more information, see the offer at the end of the books.

Conclusion

> Parents can support their child through following the steps of Emotion Coaching as outlined through this chapter and by embracing the *'Tuning into Kids®'* program. By learning how to understand your own emotions, and through this, teaching your children to understand, label and effectively express their emotions, parents can equip their children with life skills that can help them for the rest of their lives.
>
> As a result of this, parents are helping their children to develop their emotional regulation, their relationship skills, as well as expanding their understanding of emotions through the expansion of their emotional vocabulary.

Nurturing Positive Behaviour

Introduction

One of the biggest challenges parents have shared with me is supporting their children's behaviour. Parents want quick and simple solutions. Sometimes, the solution is easy, but often, it requires commitment, patience, and time.

This chapter will give you a greater understanding of what is behind your child's behaviour and some strategies to help overcome any challenging behaviours.

The Power of Perspective: Viewing Life Through a Child's Eyes

Many parents fall into the simple trap of seeing their child through the eyes of an adult. They see the world as it is for them and expect that their child sees it the same way. Unfortunately, this is far from the truth. Children have a vastly different view of the world around them than adults do. It is a world of wonder, mystery, and opportunities.

What seems small to an adult can be a huge deal to a child. This is why adults need to change their perspective and look at what is happening around their children through a lens that is responsive to their developmental level and needs. See the wonder around you as if you are looking through your child's eyes.

By doing this, you will be able to respond to their behaviour in a supportive and loving manner rather than reacting to it, and you will view their behaviour as a learning opportunity for you both.

Listening to Behaviours: The Stories They Tell

Children express themselves in more ways than just words. A child's behaviour can tell you a lot about their internal and external worlds. Frustration, boredom, tiredness and even excitement are expressed both verbally, for children who have developed communication skills, and through their behaviour.

When children are unable to communicate their needs verbally, they express this through their behaviour. This can be quite distressing for both children and parents. Understanding the story behind the behaviour can help you respond in a way that will support your child.

I had a situation many years ago. A child who we had never had behavioural issues with suddenly exploded into rage. My colleagues called me to help them as I was outside at the time. The child became very violent and was hitting and kicking me and other staff. I attempted to support the child for a little while whilst he tried to hit and kick me. Eventually, one of my colleagues said she would step in, so I did not cop all of his anger. However, it was evident they were in no mood to listen to anyone, and they were going to target anyone who was with them. Eventually, I told the other staff to supervise the other children, and I allowed myself to be the focus of their outburst. As we could not support this child, we eventually called their mother to come and collect them.

It was only after they had calmed down that I discovered they were upset because one of my colleagues had taken a packet of chips away from them at snack time and told them to eat their fruit first. Had I known this, I could have better understood what was happening with the child and been able to support them more effectively.

Recently, I was working at a different Kindergarten. When I began with the three-year-old group, one of the children would become so distressed when their mother left, that they would make themselves vomit.

The difference between this situation and the previous situation is that I knew what the trigger was, their mother leaving. I also had a greater understanding of Separation Anxiety and was able to build a strong and trusting relationship with this child.

Within a few weeks, as the children only attended kindergarten for five hours one day a week, they began to separate from their mother and come to me with little distress. Eventually, they were able to separate from their mother and move off to play without requiring my support.

The key to supporting challenging behaviour is knowing its story or root cause. Once you are aware of it, you can provide effective support and guidance to ensure your child feels heard and understood.

Seeing Beyond the Behaviour: The Story Behind the Scenes

Looking at what is going on behind the scenes, not just the behaviour, is key to understanding your child's behaviour. Look at what has been going on prior to the challenging behaviour. This will give you some idea of what is going on with your child and what it was that triggered their behaviour. Focussing on what has triggered the behaviour, shows the child that you care about them and understand that they were having a challenge with something prior to the challenging behaviour. This does not mean we accept challenging behaviour, rather we demonstrate to our child that we understand they were having difficulty and acknowledge that this led to the behaviour. It also shows that you can assist them with developing strategies to manage difficult situations.

Being aware of the circumstances leading up to the behaviour issue helps you to understand what is happening to them more deeply.

Is your child tired?

Are they feeling unwell?

Did they experience something they feel is unjust?

It may appear something small to you, but to a child it could be devastating.

I liken it to a minor injury. Imagine that you have fallen over and scraped the skin of your knee. Your graze has a diameter of about 5cm. It hurts. Now imagine, you are a five-year-old child. For an adult, this size would not cover the whole knee, but for a child, it may cover the whole knee.

This is an analogy for how children see the world around them. Something small like losing a favourite toy, can be devastating for a child. Even if you can buy an identical one.

What seems small to an adult, is actually a large thing to a child.

If you remember the Christmas holidays during your school days or going on a long road trip, you will remember how long time seemed. However, now, the same duration does not seem long enough.

Having this perspective, will help you to understand how it is to be a child and why they sometimes seem to go overboard with their behaviour.

Effective Strategies for Giving Directions

When giving your child directions, break it down into manageable parts, based upon the ability of your child to follow directions. For example, you may ask your child to get dressed, brush their teeth, and pack their bag for kindergarten; but on the contrary, you may need to break this down into one-step instructions such as put your pants on, then when this is completed, put your socks on, and so on.

Understand that the younger the child, the fewer directions they can undertake before becoming overwhelmed or distracted.

Creating realistic expectations with your instructions will help your child feel a sense of accomplishment when they are able to follow the directions you are giving. This can mitigate frustration and the need to act out and communicate through their behaviour because the expectations are too high.

Being realistic about what you want your child to do and understanding what they can do helps create healthy parameters for their learning and effective expression.

The Power of Predictability

Predictability is essential for supporting your child. When they know what is going to happen, they are less likely to exhibit challenging behaviour. Unpredictability can create anxiety in your child, which can lead to an increase in challenging and negative behaviours.

Humans are geared toward predictability. If we look at ourselves, we have created routines and schedules to make life easier. Whether it is a work, mealtime, or sleep routine, or even the routine of walking into a room and instinctively reaching for the light switch, all of these things create a sense of predictability. Children, more so, require predictability to help them learn and understand the world around them.

Predictability will help your child know what to expect and learn how to express themselves appropriately in different situations.

Predictability is a keystone to guiding your child in their learning and development.

Being Their Coach and Cheerleader

Your child is looking for you to show direction. When your child is demonstrating challenging behaviour, they have lost their way and are asking you, in the only way they can, to show them the way. They are reaching out to you through their behaviour for guidance on how to cope, what to do or what to expect. Being present with your child in these situations and available as soon as the behaviour begins or even catching it beforehand, will enable you to be able to coach your child through the situation and develop the skills to navigate them in the future.

Being present also enables you to be their cheerleader and celebrate their achievements with them. Every child wants to make their parents proud. Even the child with the most challenging behaviour reaches out to their parents, saying, "I'm here; love me."

Taking the time to teach your child the steps you want them to do will save more time than when you expect them to do something they have not mastered and, as a result, begin to show you they need help through their behaviour.

Building Accountability Through Consequences

Using consequences is especially important. This can easily teach a child the difference between acceptable and unacceptable behaviour. A consequence is something that happens because of an action or inaction. An example of a consequence is, when we throw a rock at a window, the window will break. In this situation, the consequence of the action may be that the child will need to do some chores to help pay for the replacement of the window. Punishment, on the other hand, focuses on the use of power; an example of punishment is receiving a smack or being sent to their bedroom because they broke the window. Punishment seeks to assert power and control over another, to enforce your expectations on them. Whereas consequences seek to gain an understanding of the cause and effect of actions and inactions.

Using age-appropriate consequences is essential. When a child displays challenging behaviour that you feel requires a consequence, you need to understand your child's ability to understand first. Then you need to choose an appropriate consequence that will demonstrate to your child what you expect. For example, if your child hits a sibling, a consequence could be first telling them that you are not happy with this behaviour and discussing briefly possible alternative actions for future situations, then if your child understands empathy, getting them to apologise to their sibling, followed by giving the sibling a cuddle to settle them down and spending a bit of time with them.

In this scenario, punishment could entail a smack or timeout or sending the child to their room. As you can see, the consequence would teach your child appropriate alternatives and demonstrate empathy towards the sibling. In contrast, the punishment would reinforce the negative behaviour, demonstrate power, control, and show them that physical harm is acceptable.

Consequences can be varied depending on what is happening. They can be active or passive. Active consequences are like the example discussed above, whereas passive could be something like redirecting your child's attention, distracting them with something else or diverting your attention somewhere else and responding when you see appropriate behaviour.

It will really depend upon your child and what happened as to what sort of consequence you decide to use.

Focussing on consequences over punishment, moves your own thinking towards the learning you want your child to achieve. It helps to set up healthy parameters and expectations and encourages your child to continue to explore and extend their own learning.

Modelling Calm for Your Child

Keeping yourself calm whilst your child has a tantrum is important. Remember that your child is demonstrating or communicating that they cannot cope with what is happening, and that it is not about you, even if they say it is. As you keep yourself calm, you are better equipped to keep your child safe, and when they settle down a little you will be able to begin to coach them in how to calm down and regain the control over themselves that they have lost. You can let them know it is ok to feel how they are feeling and then redirect the conversation towards how they could better manage their feelings.

When your child is in the midst of a tantrum, it is important that you keep calm. Take a few breaths and give yourself some space. Ensure that your child is safe and wait for them to calm down. You cannot reason with a child who is in a heightened state. Time is the key, time for them to calm down and become receptive to you again.

If your child is safe, step back and allow yourself to take a few deep, relaxing breaths. Imagine that you are breathing in calm and blowing out all your stress. Make a cup of tea or go to the bathroom and wash your hands and face—anything that helps you stay calm and be receptive to your child.

Once your child has calmed down, then you can begin to help them to calm down more. When they are calm, you can discuss what has happened, unless this is likely to trigger them again. It is ok to wait and discuss later, even the next day. Use a lot of I statements such as, "I felt," or "I could see," and avoid making it personal. Your goal at this point is to help your child to understand the consequences of their actions and other ways they could handle things in future.

Understanding Meltdowns

I deliberately excluded meltdowns from the previous section because they are vastly different from tantrums.

A tantrum is something a child exhibits when they are upset or angry about something as a way to express how they feel and to try to elicit a given response.

I am not saying that children are consciously using tantrums to manipulate you, they are just using a communication tool they know to communicate in the best way they can at the exact moment.

A meltdown is completely different. This usually occurs with neurodiverse children, who are overwhelmed with sensory, emotional, or other input and do not have the skills or strategies to deal with it. There is a lot going on in their brains, and they cannot cope with it, resulting in the meltdown.

All you can do is give your child a safe space to let this play out. In my experience, once the meltdown is over, children often become very sleepy or withdrawn. They may not even understand exactly what has occurred.

If you think your child is having meltdowns, rather than tantrums, it is important to speak to your child's Kindergarten Teacher or Doctor about a referral to investigate the reasons and seek a professional diagnosis.

Acknowledging and Easing Emotions

Always acknowledge your understanding of what your child is feeling and help them understand their feelings. Being the voice enables you to coach them through their feelings and teach them acceptable ways to manage them.

You can be the voice of reason pre-emptively by acknowledging the low-level emotions your child is feeling before they grow into the bigger emotions. Notice the frustration or worry early and notice the delight before it reaches excitement. Acknowledging lower-intensity emotions before they escalate into stronger ones, such as anger, anxiety, fear, or excitement, makes it easier to support your child in managing them while they are still manageable.

Cultivating Emotional Intelligence

The first thing anyone needs to do when they discover emotional intelligence is to expand their understanding of the different emotions, to expand their own emotional vocabulary.

Recently, as I was preparing for a Toastmasters Speech Contest, one of the members of my club walked in and asked how I was feeling. I immediately said, "I'm nervous." To which she replied, "No, you're excited." Being a Life Coach, she explained to me that nervousness and excitement are the same feeling but differ because of how we perceive them.

This was a huge lesson for me, as I had experienced the sensation of nervousness for many years due to my Generalised Anxiety Disorder. However, since discovering this, I have had a few moments when I have felt excited and realised that that is the feeling I was having, where, in the past, I would have acknowledged it as nervousness.

Becoming aware of the depth and variety of emotions and the different words you can use to communicate them, gives you a greater repertoire to draw upon to help your child explore the many ways of feeling.

When I discuss emotions with the children, in the beginning they recognise happy, sad, angry, and occasionally worried or scared. As time goes on, and I begin to introduce different words to them, they begin to acknowledge and use the wider emotional language they have been learning.

When you introduce new emotional language, start by using one or two different words for the emotions you are seeing. Allow them time to incorporate these, and when they are ready, introduce more words.

Every child will be different. Some may be able to handle new concepts after a few days, while others may require several weeks.

Once you have introduced the new language, you can begin with the next step, which is helping your child to recognise the emotions others are feeling. It is one thing for a child to have a strong emotional vocabulary and be able to communicate how they feel. It is another level for them to be able to recognise and understand the emotions of others and be able to communicate and show empathy for how they are feeling.

If you have already explored the chapter: *Empowering Emotional Intelligence*, you will find these strategies build on the foundation of teaching emotional intelligence.

Mindful Calming Techniques

I have already explained the importance for you to remain calm when your child is distressed or heightened. The skills, such as relaxing breaths and taking time out for yourself, are things you can also teach your child when they are receptive and calm.

Relaxing Breath

Having spent much of the last thirty years of my life meditating, I have learned that focusing on breathing is a great tool for psychological, emotional, and spiritual well-being, which also helps to foster physical health.

Wherever you are, take a moment to focus on your breath. Breathe in through your nose and out slowly through your nose. I usually do this as follows:

Breathe in 2, 3, 4. Breathe out 2, 3, 4.

Repeat this for a minute or so and notice the difference in your body and mood.

In some cases, if you are heightened, you can replace the out-breath with a strong, long out-breath through the mouth, even making a sighing sound. This can release any excess stress that you would otherwise not be able to release.

Meditation or Visualisation

Find a comfortable place to sit or lie on your back. Relax yourself with the relaxing breath as above.

Imagine you are in a calm, peaceful space that is perfect for you. Notice with your mind your physical surroundings, the sounds you can hear, the feel of the breeze, and the smell of the air.

Stay in this space for as long as you like. Five minutes is enough time if that is all you can spare. What is important is your focus.

Five minutes of focused relaxation can be as powerful as an hour of restless relaxation.

You can do this to relaxation music. Insight Timer is a fantastic, easy-to-use app that offers thousands of guided meditations and visualisations, as well as music and sounds to relax to. It also has many visualisations and sleep stories for children. You can access it from the app on your device or through the browser on the internet.

Body Scan

Body scan is an easy relaxation technique that is scientifically proven. You begin by relaxing with your breath.

Once you are relaxed, focus on your feet, and notice how they feel. Are they tense or relaxed? Tense your feet by scrunching them up and then relaxing them. As you let them go, mentally imagine all the tension leaving your feet.

Once they feel relaxed, move on.

Move up to your lower legs and notice how they feel. Then tense them by contracting the muscles and release, mentally seeing all the tension leave your lower legs.

Continue this process, moving up your body to the thighs or upper legs, buttocks, abdomen, chest, all the way up to the top of the head.

When you relax the scalp, allow yourself to sit in this space for some time, enjoying the relaxed state you have created.

Teach Your Child

Once you are familiar with these relaxation techniques, it is time to teach your child. Get them to sit or lie with you as you go through the process. Talk them through each step and allow them time to assimilate before you move on.

Encourage your child to incorporate this into their daily routine, particularly if they have stopped sleeping during the day. Twenty minutes of relaxation during the day can be the difference between a calm child who can concentrate and follow directions and a highly strung and unresponsive child.

You can take the suggestions I have mentioned above and incorporate them into other activities throughout the day.

Try taking a mindful walk with your child. Take in everything around you and enjoy the wonder of being childlike. Delve into the music and feel it around you as you sing and dance with your child.

There is no right or wrong way to relax or teach your child to relax. For some, such as myself, it is in silence or listening to music, while others need noise and a fast pace. Whatever works for you is perfect for you.

Understanding Behaviour: It is not Personal

Sometimes, our children's behaviour can be distressing not only for them but also for those around them. It is important to remember that it is not personal.

Your child is attempting to communicate something to you through their behaviour. Being responsive, rather than reactive to their behaviour, will help you to observe the behaviour with curiosity and learn how to interpret what they are communicating and why.

By removing the personalisation of the behaviour, you can examine what needs your child is not having met. You can then help them rectify the deficit so that your child can learn to cope more effectively.

Behaviour Diary

In some situations, children's behaviour can be extreme. A behaviour diary is a valuable tool for this.

A behaviour diary is a tool you can use to record the events surrounding uncharacteristic or unpleasant behaviour. Things you should note are:

Date	Time	What happened before	What triggered the behaviour	What was the behaviour	How and who it impacted	How they calmed down
16/01/2025	10:00 am	Playing with blocks inside	Tower was knocked over by a peer	Began crying and screaming, threw a block	They became very distressed and their peer moved away	Parent sat with them and soothed them with a cuddle and by talking, then helped rebuild the tower

Recording and analysing when, where, and why the behaviour occurs, as well as its impact, can help you understand it and what you can do to support your child.

If the behaviour is persistent, or you cannot work out why it is happening, and there is no improvement, please speak with your child's Kindergarten Teacher or Doctor for further support. This could be in the form of further strategies, or it may be time to consider a referral to a paediatrician for a professional diagnosis.

Understand, the behaviour is not because you are not doing the right things, but rather as a response to your child's inability to communicate their needs effectively. If you do need a referral for further assessments this is not a reflection on you as a parent. Many children struggle with their behaviour and require professional support.

Sometimes, getting that professional support is the best thing you can do for your child and you.

Conclusion

> Understanding your child's behaviour and making positive changes can help your child learn about themselves, their emotions, and how to effectively communicate this. Understanding and leading by example are two steps towards helping your child manage the challenges of being a human being in the 21st Century.

Nourishing Through Nutritious Choices

Introduction

Food is the fuel for the body. It is true that you are what you eat. We all need good nutrition and a range of different vitamins and minerals in order for our bodies to work effectively. Many parents have sought my advice on how they can get their child to eat. There is no one way to deal with a fussy eater, or a child who refuses to eat, as we are all different and there may be underlying issues that need to be addressed, however, in this chapter I will share some ideas I have given parents to help them with how to handle their child's eating habits.

Nourishing Your Body: The Essential Role of Nutrition

When we examine the human body on its basic levels, we see an extremely complicated machine with various systems that work together to form the body we see. When we eat processed food that is low in nutrition, we introduce the wrong things into the system, which can have a flow-on effect creating imbalances within the body.

We can use the scenario of a car to illustrate this. A car runs on petrol and requires the petrol to fuel the engine to make it go. If, instead, we put water into the petrol tank, the engine will not work. If we put low-quality fuel into the car, the engine will run, however, it will not run as efficiently. When we put high-quality fuel in that is appropriate for that vehicle, the car runs smoothly and requires less maintenance as there is less wear on the mechanical parts of the car.

The human body is similar, though even more complex than the car. Poor quality food, such as takeaway foods, processed and packaged foods and sugary drinks, are low in nutrition while being high in harmful ingredients such as saturated and trans fats, processed sugars, colourings, and preservatives, which the body does not recognise as 'food'. Whereas real 'nude' foods, such as fresh fruit and vegetables, lean meats, fish, eggs, and dairy are more natural sources of the vitamins, minerals, and amino acids the human body requires to function optimally.

Nourishing Through Nutritious Choices

Portion Size: Key to Nurturing Healthy Kids

When I talk to parents about helping them to get their children to eat, the first thing I usually discuss is portion size.

Your empty stomach is the size of your fist, and this goes the same for your children. The stomach has the capacity to stretch as it is filled with food. You can use the size of your child's fist as a guide to help you gauge how much food to put on their plate or in their lunch box.

When considering how much to put in your child's lunchbox, I recommend that you divide the food into two or three portions, depending on how long your child will be in Kindergarten and how many mealtimes and snack breaks they will have.

Monitor how much food is left in your child's lunch box when they come home and modify the amount you put in next time based on how much is eaten or not eaten. If you are concerned your child is not eating enough at Kindergarten, speak to their teacher so they are aware of your concern and can monitor how your child is eating at Kinder.

Children will not starve themselves. If they are active in play, they may forget to eat unless they are prompted to, but they will not starve. They may go hungry for a little while if they do not like something, but they will eventually eat well before they reach the point of starvation, unless, of course, there is no food available. Keep making healthy food available to your child, and they will eat when they are hungry enough!

Do not worry too much if your child does not eat what you deem is 'enough' on one single day. Some days your child will eat more, whilst other days they will eat less. When they are going through growth spurts their appetite may increase, when they are sick it may decrease. It is the overall input of food that matters. Observe how much they eat over a period of a week. If the amount of food is low, and you are concerned, speak to your doctor or child health nurse.

If over a period of days or a week your child is taking in sufficient nutrients, then they will remain healthy and well. If the nutrient intake is not sufficient or of poor quality, this may lead to health concerns.

A rule of thumb is to offer smaller portions and increase the portions as your child's appetite grows. This is easier to manage at home than when eating out of the home. For example, when preparing a meal at home, put a smaller portion than you think your child could eat on their plate and when they are finished or almost finished, offer them a second serve, or ask them what they would like more of.

By offering serving sizes that your child can finish, you are empowering your child by enabling them to feel the satisfaction of being able to finish their meal and ask or accept more.

Introducing new foods requires a different strategy, which I will discuss next.

Introducing New Foods: A Gentle Approach to Expanding Your Child's Diet

Many parents raise the concern that their child will not try new foods or the foods they would like them to eat more of. This can be frustrating for the parent and for the child.

Nourishing Through Nutritious Choices

When introducing a new food to your child, it is important to do it gradually and gently. Just like when introducing a new food to a baby, do not give your child a large portion. When introducing a new food to a baby, you introduce one food at a time and keep it to small portions until you know how the baby responds to the new food. Similarly, this should be done with children when introducing new foods.

Keep the new food portion small and offer it regularly to your child. When they can eat it without any objections, you can introduce it as a staple in their diet.

Portion size is extremely important for new foods you are introducing to your child. I like to use the example of peas when discussing adding new foods. When I was young, I could not eat peas by chewing them. I did not like the texture of mushy peas; they made me feel ill. I began to swallow them whole to please my parents. I also came to learn that if I noticed Mum and Dad were not watching me, I could pick my plate up and hold it up high and say, "I'm finished" and then go scrape my plate into the dog bowl. Over time, I overcame this aversion to peas, but it took a long time.

When introducing any new food, for example, peas, do not put a full portion on your child's plate. Put a small portion, such as two or three peas on their plate. If they do not tolerate them on their plate, put them on a separate small plate on the table so they can look at them, touch, smell, and taste them to get them used to the smell, taste, and texture of the peas. If your child tolerates them, put them on their plate but keep the serve to a small number. Once they are able to eat all of those peas, then offer some more. If they do want more, give them another serve of two or three, until they have had enough. Once they are tolerating two or three, increase the number slowly over a few days, until you get to a small spoon serve.

Regardless of the food, keep the serving size small until your child shows they want more and enjoy the food. Then, you can work up to a child-size serving. Smaller serving sizes set your child up for success, as they are more likely to eat two or three peas than a spoonful. They also enable your child to request more serves as they begin to enjoy the food you are introducing.

It is also useful to note that it may take twenty or more attempts before children accept a new food. It can be a good idea to put new foods on communal plates that everyone can serve themselves from. This way your child will see others enjoying the food, and they will eventually want to try it and see how it tastes.

Everyday vs. Sometimes Food: How Your Choices Shape Your Child's Eating Habits

Educating your child about 'everyday' food and 'sometimes' food is also important. This goes beyond just telling them; you need to demonstrate this through your own eating habits as well and lead by example. It will not work telling your child that chocolate or chips are sometimes foods if you are eating a block of chocolate or a bag of chips every day. If you demonstrate eating a healthy balanced diet, with the occasional treat, then your child will learn from you that this is the best choice to follow and be less inclined to crave or demand sweets and treats.

I recently attended a PD Day (Professional Development Day) on Celebrating Diversity. The presenter did a quick little activity to

Nourishing Through Nutritious Choices

show how our actions are greater than words. She had everyone make a fist and hold it up in the air. She placed her fist against her cheek and then asked us to put our fist on our chin. The majority of people placed their fist against their cheek instead of their chin as she instructed. This was done for a different purpose than this book, however the message is the same.

Your children follow your actions and words; however, actions are easier to understand and follow and have a greater impact on a developing child.

Another example is if you establish rules around your child's use of devices like the iPhone or iPad. However, if you are on your device for lengthy periods of time, your child will follow your actions, and this will inevitably create challenges around managing how and when your child uses their devices.

If you want to encourage positive eating habits and healthy food choices for your child, you need to make these same choices yourself. Not only will this make you a fantastic role model for your child, but you will also benefit from the benefits of healthy eating.

Most packaged food, even those marketed as heathy for children, have high sugar, saturated and trans fats, excess salt, colourings, and preservatives. If you are buying these types of products, make sure you check the packaging and do your own investigation into the chemicals and preservatives in your foods. A good resource to access is the Chemical Maze book by Bill Statham, which has thousands of preservatives for foods and cosmetics and their possible health impacts. There is also an app you can download to your device called "Chemical Maze".

I once heard a chef on TV say, "When you go to the supermarket, shop on the periphery." Fresh produce, meat, dairy, and frozen goods are all in the outside aisles. These foods are less processed and have fewer additives. If you focus your shopping in these areas and minimise shopping in the middle aisles, you will have a much healthier shopping experience.

Alternatively, you can go to the local fresh food market to buy your fruit and vegetables, the local butcher and delicatessen for meats, and the fish shop for seafood. Farm gates and farmers markets are also a fantastic source of fresh produce, and your children can see where the produce is grown. Not only will you have access to what is in season and higher quality, but you will also be supporting the local economy directly.

I embraced this choice for a year before the publication of this book, and its profound positive impact on my physical and psychological health has been evident.

Mealtimes: Creating Connections and Mindful Eating Habits

Eating meals together as a family is essential to supporting good eating habits in your child. Not only does it create a connected mood within the family, demonstrating a sense of togetherness, but it is also a wonderful opportunity for your child to learn from you appropriate table manners and practices. Eating at the table and switching off the television and other devices add to the atmosphere of togetherness and encourage individuals to talk and communicate about their day. This builds upon the relationships you have already developed.

Nourishing Through Nutritious Choices

In the Kindergarten setting, staff always sit with the children to eat, or if they have already eaten, they sit with the children to model and support social interactions.

Creating a positive atmosphere around the consumption of meals takes the focus away from the food for children who are fussy or picky eaters and shifts their focus to the social aspects of the meal. As humans are social creatures, we need that social connection and mealtime is a perfect time for families to come together to debrief about the day, and get to know what everyone has been doing, whilst at the same time enjoying a healthy meal together.

There is another reason to turn off the devices whilst eating, and that is to create an environment where you and your children can have the opportunity to eat mindfully. Mindful eating is when you focus all your attention on the process of eating. Looking at and smelling the food, observing the colours and textures, tasting the food on the tip of the tongue and chewing the food thoroughly. Not only does mindfulness give you a new outlook on the food you are eating, but it also can help you feel full on a smaller portion, as it takes about 20 minutes for your stomach to register satiety. You do not need to eat a whole meal mindfully; you can use the lulls in the conversation as an opportunity to direct your focus towards your meal. It is helpful to put your knife and fork down between mouthfuls and ensure that you chew each mouthful until it is soft before you swallow the food. Your child will see this, and eventually, they will begin to copy your example.

Conscious Parenting

Meal Preparation: Creating Culinary Adventures with Your Child

As with anything you want to teach your child, getting them involved is a fantastic way to foster a healthy relationship with food.

When you are making your shopping list for your meals for the week, talk to your child about what you are planning to cook and what you will need to buy. Take your child with you when you go shopping for food. Encourage your child to help select the foods that you have on your shopping list. For example, ask them to pick five apples, three onions, four potatoes and put them in the trolley or basket.

When you get home, ask your child to help put the food away in its appropriate place. For example, the fruit will go in a fruit bowl on the table, the vegetables in the crisper in the fridge, and the frozen goods in the freezer. Any engagement with food, particularly foods your child is reluctant to eat, is a positive engagement for your child.

When it is time to prepare a meal or pack your child's lunch for Kindergarten, involve your child. Ask them to help wash the fruit and vegetables, and if they are capable, have them help you cut them up. Ask your child what they would like to take for lunch. Depending on their ability to make choices, you may want to give them the choice of two items.

Involving your child in food preparation first gets them involved and familiar with the food. Second, it exposes them to foods they are hesitant to try. Third, it also supports their sense of agency, which is their ability to make choices and decisions that affect them. Helping your child make decisions about food and food preparation will help them understand and explore food more than just having a plate placed in front of them or a lunch box in their bag.

From Seed to Plate: The Joy of Vegetable Gardening with Kids

If your home has the capacity, making a vegetable patch is a fantastic way to get kids interested in vegetables. You can go as simple as a couple of pots or planter boxes, or as big as converting a large area of your back or front yard into a vegetable garden. Involving your child in preparing the soil and then selecting the seeds or seedlings to plant is a fun way for them to learn about the foods they eat.

In my time as a Kindergarten teacher, I have found that most children will at least taste something they have grown themselves. Some will still not like it, while others will dive right in and enjoy eating the fruits of their labour. There really is something about the engagement and satisfaction children get from planting and tending a garden that will often encourage them to try something they have never eaten before.

I have often bought a selection of different vegetables, and used them to guide discussions about different vegetables, how they grow and where they grow. I will then cut them up and make them into a tasting tray, where children are encouraged to try the different vegetables. When a child chooses something and they do not like it, I acknowledge this and allow them to put it into the compost bin. It is better to let them smell, lick, and taste the food, and then throw it away if they do not want to eat it, rather than force them to eat something they do not like.

Children will always find a way to avoid eating something they do not like, as I did.

Involving your child in vegetable growing not only teaches them how to grow vegetables but also gives them some ownership. They are more likely to try something they have grown than something that is placed on a plate in front of them.

When I was young, my father would grow vegetables, and I still remember going out with him to harvest the peas from the vegetable garden. It is amazing how they never made it into the house. There is nothing better than harvesting your own fresh peas and eating them straight off the plant.

Fostering a Positive Food Relationship: Ditching Rewards

Avoid using food as a reward or a punishment, as this can create a negative view of food and an unhealthy relationship with eating. With the rising prevalence of food-related disorders and obesity, you want to create a positive relationship with food for your children. Even using food as a reward can create a negative relationship, as it teaches the child that if I am 'good,' I can have a particular food, but if I am 'bad,' I cannot.

We want children to be able to make positive choices about the foods they eat, and this starts with the relationship you foster with your child regarding food. Remember, food is the fuel that runs our bodies. Using it negatively creates a negative relationship, which we want to avoid. By keeping the concept of food as fuel rather than a recreational resource, reward, or punishment, you can foster a positive relationship with food in your child.

Conclusion

Though it can be challenging for parents to get their children to eat, particularly healthy foods, a consistent approach of small servings, regular exposure, and a positive relationship with a variety of foods will help parents establish healthy eating habits in their children and guide them to have a healthy and positive relationship with the food they eat.

As a result, your child can experience better health, play and learn more effectively, have more sustained energy, and potentially fewer bouts of illness.

Cultivating Restful Sleep Habits

Introduction

Bedtime can be a challenge for many parents, however it is an important part of your child's routine, as it allows your child to grow and rejuvenate and supports their overall health and well-being.

In this chapter, parents will learn why sleep is important and some tips for creating a welcoming sleep environment for their children.

The Vital Role of Sleep in Child Development

Bedtime and sleep, like all other areas of a child's life, require boundaries and predictability. When a child has an irregular bedtime and sleep routine, or no routine at all, then children lose important sleep. A child who is allowed to stay up until they fall asleep will continue to fight the sleep urge until it overwhelms them, and they will not receive the amount nor the quality of sleep that they require for their growing and developing body. An ineffective bedtime and sleep routine can lead to behavioural problems as well as illness if not rectified.

If parents have concerns about their child's sleeping, they can speak to their doctor or Maternal Health Nurse for support and, where necessary, a referral to a sleep clinic.

Understanding Your Child's Sleep Needs

According to the Raising Children Network, children between five and eleven years of age need between nine and eleven hours of sleep, including naps if they have them. This means that a five-year-old who gets up at 7:00 am needs to be in bed no later than 9:00 pm for a ten-hour sleep. You will learn how long your child sleeps, whether they sleep closer to the nine hours a night or to the eleven hours.

Knowing the time they wake up, or you get them up, you can now count back the required number of hours. Depending on what time your child goes to bed, you need to then count back a further two hours or so to set a time for your child's bedtime routine so that you have plenty of time for bathing, brushing teeth, and stories, or whatever your child's bedtime routine is so that they are ready for lights out at the designated bedtime.

Having determined what time your child needs to go to bed based on how long they sleep and when they get up or are woken in the morning, you can now focus on establishing their bedtime routine, as discussed in the previous section of this chapter.

I once had a three-year-old child in my Kindergarten group. They always arrived over an hour after the session began, and within an hour this child would be rubbing their eyes and would find it extremely difficult to self-regulate throughout the day. When I discussed this with their parent, I asked them what time the child went to bed. They reported that the child went to bed around 11:00 pm and I told them this was too late for their age and explained how much sleep they required, quoting the Raising Children Network figures. They said that the child would wake around 12:00 am if they went to bed at 8:00 pm so they let them stay up until they fell asleep.

Unfortunately, the parent was not open to my suggestions, even though I offered suggestions like creating a bedtime routine or even speaking to their doctor for support. All I could do was offer as much support as possible and make sure there were quiet areas where the child could rest during the day if they became too tired.

You can see the children who have a good, stable bedtime and sleep routine. They are refreshed and eager to engage in the day. Children like the one I have just discussed who do not have an effective bedtime and sleep routine often present as tired, restless, and unable to cope with even the smallest changes or interruptions to their day.

This is why it is important to understand how much sleep your child needs and base their bedtime routine on this amount of sleep; knowing that your child will sleep more when they are unwell or going through a growth spurt and less at times when there is something exciting happening such as their birthday or other significant event in their life.

It is all about setting up the parameters for a solid and predictable bedtime and sleep routine, which will create positive sleeping habits and support your child to recognise their own need for sleep.

Establishing a Predictable Bedtime Routine for Better Sleep

Having a predictable and stable routine is essential for establishing or re-establishing a good sleep routine for your child. Having a set schedule or routine you follow every night, will enable your child to anticipate and feel more comfortable with preparing to go to sleep. Minimising device use during the two hours prior to bedtime is essential.

Devices like phones and tablets give off blue light, which interrupts and suppresses the production of melatonin, the hormone that regulates the sleep/wake cycle.

Having a routine such as bath time, putting on pyjamas, brushing teeth, story, soft music, and lights out that you follow every night helps your child to understand what is coming next and will work towards developing healthy sleeping patterns.

Predictability also helps decrease any anxiety your child may feel about going to sleep, such as whether they will sleep alone in their own bed in their own room or whether there will be a night light.

If you have an established routine, you may choose to keep it or tweak it with what you have learnt in this chapter, whereas, if you do not have an established bedtime routine, you may choose to establish one such as in the table below.

Time	Routine
6:00 pm	Eat dinner
6:30 pm	Have a bath
7:00 pm	Put pyjamas on and brush teeth
7:15 pm	Read stories
7:50 pm	Finish reading stories
7:55 pm	Last hugs and kisses
8:00 pm	Say goodnight and turn light off

This is not an exhaustive example; it is just a sample that you can use to create a routine that is suitable and effective for you and your child.

Creating a Calming Bedroom: Minimising Distractions for Better Sleep

Sit on your child's bed. Or even better, if you can, sit on the floor. Have a look around their bedroom. Take in everything you see. Are there pictures or furnishings all over the walls? Are there toys scattered about? Are things hanging from the roof?

Take a good long look. Once you have, imagine that you are your child's age, and you are getting ready for bed. What is the first thing that comes to your mind?

Does the room help you feel calm, relaxed, and ready for bed, or is it busy and exciting, encouraging you to explore and play?

If the room feels busy and exciting, what can you remove to make it feel calming and relaxing? Can you minimise the pictures and displays on the walls or put toys in a cupboard or toy box? Are the colours bright and stimulating or soft and soothing?

Minimising visual clutter removes distractions from your child's view, making the room more inviting for sleep. On the other hand, a room full of toys and things to look at will be very stimulating and entice your child to play.

Consider the paint on the walls as well. Bright colours are more stimulating and encourage play, whereas softer or pastel colours are more soothing and often used to set a calmer tone in a room.

Another consideration: if you have trees just outside your child's window, consider whether you can prune these back so that they do not tap or scratch on the window or the roof.

Conclusion

Creating a predictable bedtime and sleep routine is an important and simple thing all parents can do for their children. Parents can take some time to determine the amount of time their children sleep and use this information to create the sleep routine. They can also consider the arrangement of the child's bedroom to help support healthy, positive sleep habits in their children.

Conclusion

As I reflect on the journey of writing this book, I am utterly amazed at the insights and practices that have come together. Revisiting these chapters has reinforced the principles and approaches that have guided me throughout my career in education.

Some chapters flowed effortlessly from my fingertips as if they were waiting to be written, while others presented challenges that shaped the final result. Yet, each chapter came together in the only way it could, forming a cohesive guide for parents and caregivers.

This book began as a collection of workshops I created for parents in early 2024. Since then, so much has changed. I have grown as a person and embraced new perspectives, which are woven into the pages of *Conscious Parenting*.

Conscious Parenting

When life challenges us, we have two choices: to give up or to persevere. I am deeply grateful that I chose to push forward. Completing this book has been a deeply fulfilling achievement, and I hope it serves as a meaningful resource for families.

Throughout this book, you have discovered strategies, tips, and tools to help nurture your child and create an enjoyable start to their formal education. From choosing the right resources and easing separation anxiety to fostering positive eating habits, becoming an emotion coach, and teaching emotional intelligence, these ideas are here to empower you.

Everything you have read is possible when approached with curiosity and an open mind. You and your child are the true beneficiaries of these strategies, equipped with tools to navigate Kindergarten, childhood, and beyond.

As I prepare to sign off, I want to share a final thought with you, one that came to me as I was completing my previous book *The KISS of Taoway*, "Be the Change you want to See." Be the change that your child deserves and set them up for success.

About the Author

With over twenty years of experience as a Kindergarten Teacher, John brings both heart and a wealth of knowledge to the field of early childhood education. Having struggled as a student himself, John discovered his passion for learning and development upon entering the field. This journey allowed him to explore the complexities of the human condition, which guided him throughout his career.

John views life as an ever-evolving adventure where we continuously expand our understanding and strive to do better. He has dedicated his career to fostering positive, compassionate, and developmentally enriching environments for young children. John holds a Bachelor of Arts, a Graduate Diploma in Early Childhood Education, a Graduate Diploma in Primary Education, and a Diploma of Holistic Counselling. He is also a passionate Toastmaster.

As a father of three, John is currently pursuing a Graduate Certificate in Education and Development with RMIT. Outside of his work with children, John actively supports the Berwick and Lynbrook Toastmasters Clubs in the City of Casey. Through Toastmasters, he has honed his public speaking skills and taken on various leadership roles that have further enriched his abilities.

John is also a committed member of the Seaford Spiritualist Church and a developing Trance Medium. He serves as the Healing Coordinator and contributes through opening and closing prayers, meditations, and reflective words throughout the service.

Beyond teaching, John is dedicated to helping others become the best version of themselves, whether they are children, parents, or colleagues. His previous book, *KISS of Toaway: A Father's Journey from Anxiety to Enlightenment* (2021), reflects his personal journey. While he may not yet have found full enlightenment, he is well on his way. Through the support of his Clinical Nutritionist, Counsellor and his commitment to self-care, John has successfully managed his Generalised Anxiety Disorder.

John's guiding principle, "Be the change you want to see," is something he lives by every day. He believes that as long as we keep moving forward, it does not matter how long it takes to reach our destination. The journey itself is the true teacher, offering wisdom long after we arrive.

Acknowledgements

**Professor Sophie Havighurst and Ann Harley –
Creators of Tuning into Kids®**

I would like to express my heartfelt gratitude to Professor. Sophie Havighurst and Ann Harley, the visionary creators of *Tuning into Kids®*. It was a true honour to complete my facilitation training with you in 2023. Thank you for the opportunity to share the remarkable impact of your work, which has profoundly shaped my journey as an Early Childhood Professional.

Christine Goritchan – Bachelor Education and Graduate Diploma of Education

Christine, I want to express my deepest gratitude for your unwavering support and love. Your help in editing several chapters of this book was invaluable, but even more so, I am profoundly grateful for the role you have played in helping me discover the man I am today. Sincerely, thank you.

Iryna Chapman

Iryna, thank you for challenging me to pause and think critically about the 'Nourishing Through Nutritious Choices' chapter. Your insightful feedback and thought-provoking questions have enriched this section, ensuring it resonates deeply with readers. I am truly grateful for your guidance and support.

Lauren Michel – Clinical Nutritionist

Lauren, I extend my deepest gratitude for your insightful and thorough editing and feedback on the 'Nourishing Through Nutritious Choices' chapter. Your keen eye and thoughtful suggestions have brought clarity and depth to this section, ensuring its message is both impactful and practical. Beyond your contribution to this book, your guidance as my clinical nutritionist has been life changing. The positive impact you have had on my personal health—helping me understand the importance of healthy eating and discovering the foods that are best for my unique needs—cannot be overstated. Your expertise, encouragement, and unwavering support have not only enriched this chapter but have also profoundly influenced

Acknowledgements

my well-being. Thank you for being an invaluable part of both my writing and health journeys.

Kaylene Ledgar – Holistic Life and Communication Coach

Kaylene, thank you for inspiring me to pursue my lifelong dream of writing. You played a pivotal role in my journey to becoming a published author. Your simple yet profound question, 'What's holding you back?' when I mentioned that someone had asked if I was writing a book, resonated deeply and gave me the courage to take the leap. I am immensely grateful for the thoughtful feedback you provided on the chapters we discussed and for your unwavering support throughout this journey. Your encouragement has been, and will always be, invaluable to me.

Vandana Verma – Secondary School Teacher

Vandana, my heartfelt thanks for your expertise in editing the 'Empowering Emotional Intelligence' chapter. Your thoughtful input and mindfulness have truly elevated this section, ensuring its message is both clear and impactful. Thank you for your invaluable support.

Victoria – my editor

I would like to express my heartfelt gratitude to my editor, Victoria, for her unwavering dedication and thought-provoking contributions to my manuscript. Her insightful feedback not only sharpened my work but also encouraged me at a time when I needed it most. Victoria's support has been invaluable, and her guidance has inspired me to bring out the best in this project. Thank you for being an integral part of this journey.

To my family, friends, colleagues, and supporters,

I want to express my heartfelt thanks to each and every one of you who has supported me throughout the journey of writing *Conscious Parenting*. The feedback I have received from all of you has been profound, and it has reinforced the importance of persevering through challenging times to complete this book. I recognise that at times I may have 'chewed your ear off' talking about the concept of this book, especially for those of you who do not work in the early childhood field. I am grateful for your patience and unwavering support throughout this process.

Sincerely, thank you.

References
list of references or sources and citations

The Magic of Kindergarten
- Ralph Waldo Emerson "It's not the destination, it's the journey."
- Universal access to early childhood education
  - https://www.aph.gov.au/About_Parliament/Parliamentary_Departments/Parliamentary_Library/pubs/rp/rp1314/QG/ChildhoodEducatAccess

Ready, Set, Kindergarten
- Play, move, improve.
  - http://www.playmoveimprove.com.au/

Kindergarten – New Beginnings
- No Jab No Play for early childhood education and care services | health.vic.gov.au
  - https://www.health.vic.gov.au/immunisation/no-jab-no-play

Separation Made Smooth
- Monash Health Allied Health
  - https://monashhealth.org/services/allied-health/

The Power of Play
- Victorian Early Years Learning and Development Framework
  - https://www.education.vic.gov.au/Documents/childhood/providers/edcare/veyldframework.pdf
- Google Scholar search Benefit of play in children's development
  - https://scholar.google.com.au/scholar?hl=en&as_sdt=0%2C5&q=benefit+of+play+in+children%27s+development&oq=benefit+of+play+
- Maria Montessori "Play is the work of the child."

Empowering Emotional Intelligence
- *Raising Emotionally Intelligent Children* by John Gottman
- Tuning into Kids
  - https://tuningintokids.org.au/
- Emotional Intelligence in Leadership: Why It's Important (hbs.edu)
  - https://online.hbs.edu/blog/post/emotional-intelligence-in-leadership

list of references or sources and citations

Tuning into Kids®

- Tuning into Kids®
  - https://tuningintokids.org.au/
- Relationships Australia
  - https://www.relationshipsvictoria.org.au/child-parenting-courses/

Nurturing Positive Behaviour

- Insight Timer
  - https://insighttimer.com/

Nourishing Through Nutritious Choices

- The Chemical Maze by Bill Statham
  - https://chemicalmaze.com/

Cultivating Restful Sleep Habits

- Raising Children Network
  - https://raisingchildren.net.au/

Special Offers

- Relationships Australia
  - https://www.relationshipsvictoria.org.au/child-parenting-courses/

Speaker Bio

John Ledgar is a seasoned Kindergarten Teacher with over 25 years of experience in the Education sector. With a deep passion for nurturing children's development and empowering parents, John has become a trusted guide for families navigating the complexities of modern parenting.

As the author of Conscious Parenting: Insights and Wisdom from a Veteran Kindergarten Teacher, John blends decades of classroom expertise with practical strategies to help parents foster meaningful connections with their children. His engaging and relatable approach inspires confidence in parents and carers, offering tools to nurture children's emotional, social, and cognitive growth.

Beyond the classroom, John is an accomplished public speaker and active member of Toastmasters, where he has honed his ability to captivate and inspire audiences. Known for his authentic storytelling and actionable insights, John delivers memorable presentations that resonate with diverse groups.

John invites individuals, schools, and organisations to connect and explore the transformative power of Conscious Parenting. Whether you are looking for a keynote speaker for your next event, a workshop facilitator, or a collaborator on parenting initiatives, John brings a wealth of knowledge, passion, and practicality to every engagement.

Contact John Ledgar today to learn how he can bring his unique insights to your next event or initiative. Together, let us inspire positive change for families and communities.

Special Offers

I am a passionate educator, author, and public speaker with over 20 years of experience in Early Childhood Education. I hold a Bachelor of Arts with a major in History, Graduate Diplomas in Early Childhood and Primary Education, a Diploma of Holistic Counselling, and Tuning into Kids® facilitation certificate. Throughout my career, I have been dedicated to empowering children, parents, and educators through meaningful learning and guidance.

As a veteran Kindergarten Teacher and a father, I have witnessed the profound joys and challenges of parenting. My firsthand experiences, combined with my commitment to fostering emotional intelligence and resilience in children, inspired me to write *Conscious Parenting: Insights and Wisdom from a Veteran Kindergarten Teacher.* This book blends practical strategies with heartfelt stories to equip parents with tools for cultivating strong, empathetic connections with their children.

In addition to my extensive teaching background, I am actively involved in Toastmasters, where I have refined my public speaking and leadership skills. I have a deep passion for engaging audiences through workshops and talks, sharing insights on parenting, child development, and emotional well-being.

My approach emphasises compassion, integrity, and the power of creating nurturing environments for both children and their families. Through my book and speaking engagements, I inspire parents and educators to embrace the challenges of modern parenting with confidence and intention.

When I am not writing or speaking, I enjoy exploring the outdoors, supporting community initiatives, and collaborating with others to share knowledge and promote growth.

I am available to speak at events, workshops, and conferences. Whether you want to spark meaningful conversations about parenting or provide actionable tools for families or professionals, my insights will inspire and empower your audience.

My passion lies in supporting people—whether they are parents, colleagues, children, or anyone open and receptive to my guidance. Over the years, I have created a variety of short workshops for parents, many of which served as inspiration for my book.

As a special offer for my supporters, I am giving back to those who support me by purchasing my book Conscious Parenting. Below are a few exclusive offers for parents who want to take advantage of this opportunity. When booking or ordering one of the following, please use the code word "Conscious Parenting".

Special Offers

✡ Special Offer: Free Customised Social Story for Separation Anxiety! ✡

Claim your free customised social story today and help your child navigate separation anxiety with ease!

Navigating separation anxiety can be a challenging experience for both parents and children. As a Kindergarten Teacher with over 20 years of experience, I understand how important it is to support children through this emotional journey.

I am pleased to offer you a **customised free social story** designed specifically to help your child cope with separation anxiety. This personalised story will address your child's unique feelings and experiences, providing them with comfort and understanding.

What is a Social Story? A social story is a narrative that helps children understand and manage their emotions in specific situations. In this case, the story will focus on:

- Recognising feelings of anxiety or fear during separations.
- Understanding that separation is a normal part of life.
- Exploring strategies for coping with separation in a positive way.
- Reassuring them of your love and support, even when apart.

To receive your free customised social story, simply:
1. Contact me via https://linktr.ee/johnledgar.
2. Share a brief description of your child's experiences with separation anxiety and any specific elements you would like included.

Let us work together to empower your child with the tools they need to feel more secure and confident during separations.

✡ Discounted One-Hour Consultation for Parents! ✡

Are you a parent navigating the challenges of raising a child? I understand how overwhelming it can be to face concerns or issues regarding your child's development, behaviour, or emotional well-being. That is why I am excited to offer you a **discounted one-hour consultation** tailored to your needs.

During this session, we will explore your concerns and work together to find practical strategies that align with conscious parenting principles. Whether you are looking for guidance on communication, discipline, or nurturing your child's emotional health, I am here to support you.

✡ To claim your discounted consultation, simply reach out by visiting my Linktree at the end of this section and let us start the conversation! ✡

Let us embark on this journey together to foster a deeper connection with your child and cultivate a nurturing environment for their growth.

✡ Special Offer for Parents: Free First Session of Tuning into Kids® Program ✡

As a dedicated Kindergarten Teacher with over 20 years of experience, I've explored many professional development avenues, but nothing has compared to the transformative journey

Special Offers

I experienced through the Tuning into Kids® Facilitator Training in 2023. This evidence-based, emotion-focused parenting program, developed by Professor Sophie Havighurst and Ann Harley in 1999, ignited my passion for emotional intelligence—a topic I have been exploring for years.

I am excited to share this journey with you! As a special thank you for purchasing my book, **"Conscious Parenting: Insights and Wisdom from a Veteran Kindergarten Teacher,"** I am offering a **free first session** of the Tuning into Kids® program. This free session will be applied once enrolment is confirmed, and payment for the remaining five sessions has been received.

What you will learn in this program:

Emotional Intelligence: Understand the importance of recognising and managing emotions.

Emotion Coaching: Discover techniques to help your child navigate their feelings.

Emotion Talk Time: Learn how to engage in meaningful conversations about emotions.

Meta-emotions: Explore how your feelings about feelings impact your parenting.

Parenting Styles: Examine different approaches, including Dismissive and Emotion Coaching styles.

Empathy Development: Foster empathy in your child and enhance their emotional vocabulary.

The program includes a variety of engaging formats, such as:

- Presentations
- Group Discussions
- Role Plays
- Interactive Activities
- Whole and Small Group Work

By participating, you will equip yourself with practical tools to support your child in understanding, managing, and expressing their emotions positively.

To complete the program, you will need to attend at least four out of the six sessions, earning a participation certificate upon completion.

Important Note: While I am here to guide you, I am not a trained therapist and cannot sign off on court-appointed participants. If you need to participate due to a court order, please visit Relationships Australia for additional support options.

Claim your free first session today and embark on this empowering journey together!

Let Us Connect

Thank you for prioritising your growth as a parent and enhancing the lives of your children. If you have any questions about *"Conscious Parenting" or* the Tuning into Kids® program or would like to explore how I can support you, I am here to help!

Special Offers

You can reach out through my Linktree account: https://linktr.ee/johnledgar.

Here, you can connect with me on social media or send your inquiries via email.

You might want to connect with me if you:

- Want to discuss strategies for managing separation anxiety or other emotional challenges your child may face.
- Are interested in personalised support tailored to your child's unique needs.
- Have questions about the Tuning into Kids® program and how it can benefit your family.
- Would like to learn more about my other services, including workshops and consultations.
- Want to share your experiences or seek guidance in your parenting journey.

I look forward to connecting with you and supporting you in nurturing your child's emotional well-being!

Notes

www.ingramcontent.com/pod-product-compliance
Lightning Source LLC
Chambersburg PA
CBHW020419080526
44584CB00014B/1401